Greek Cooking

Greek Cooking

The classic recipes of Greece made simple – 70 authentic
traditional dishes from the heart of the Mediterranean
shown step-by-step in 240 glorious photographs

Rena Salaman and Jan Cutler

southwater

This edition is published by Southwater, an imprint of Anness Publishing Ltd, Hermes House, 88–89 Blackfriars Road, London SE1 8HA; tel. 020 7401 2077; fax 020 7633 9499

www.southwaterbooks.com; www.annesspublishing.com

If you like the images in this book and would like to investigate using them for publishing, promotions or advertising, please visit our website www.practicalpictures.com for more information.

UK agent: The Manning Partnership Ltd;
tel. 01225 478444; fax 01225 478440; sales@manning-partnership.co.uk
UK distributor: Grantham Book Services Ltd;
tel. 01476 541080; fax 01476 541061; orders@gbs.tbs-ltd.co.uk
North American agent/distributor: National Book Network;
tel. 301 459 3366; fax 301 429 5746; www.nbnbooks.com
Australian agent/distributor: Pan Macmillan Australia;
tel. 1300 135 113; fax 1300 135 103; customer.service@macmillan.com.au
New Zealand agent/distributor: David Bateman Ltd; tel. (09) 415 7664; fax (09) 415 8892

ETHICAL TRADING POLICY
Because of our ongoing ecological investment programme, you, as our customer, can have the pleasure and reassurance of knowing that a tree is being cultivated on your behalf to naturally replace the materials used to make the book you are holding. For further information about this scheme, go to www.annesspublishing.com/trees.

Publisher: Joanna Lorenz
Senior Managing Editor: Conor Kilgallon
Editors: Jennifer Mussett, Lucy Doncaster and Elizabeth Woodland
Editorial Reader: Rosanna Fairhead
Recipes: Catherine Atkinson, Jacqueline Clark, Trish Davies, Roz Denny, Joanna Farrow, Jenni Fleetwood, Christine Ingram, Lucy Knox, Maggie Mayhew, Keith Richmond, Rena Salaman, Jennie Shapter, Jenny White, Kate Whiteman
Photographers: Tim Auty, Martin Brigdale, Nicky Dowey, Gus Filgate, Michelle Garrett, John Heseltine, Janine Hosegood, William Lingwood, Craig Robertson
Stylist: Helen Trent
Food Stylists: Jacqueline Clark, Joanna Farrow, Carole Handslip, Lucy McKelvie, Emma Patmore, Annabel Ford, Bridget Sargeson, Jennie Shapter, Carol Tenant, Linda Tubby, Sunil Vijayakar, Jenny White
Designer: Graham Webb
Cover Designer: Terry Jeavons
Production Controller: Steve Lang

Previously published as part of a larger volume, *The Food and Cooking of Greece*

Main front cover image shows Fresh Green Beans with Tomato Sauce – for recipe, see page 64

NOTES
Bracketed terms are intended for American readers.
For all recipes, quantities are given in both metric and imperial measures and, where appropriate, in standard cups and spoons. Follow one set of measures, but not a mixture, because they are not interchangeable.
Standard spoon and cup measures are level.
1 tsp = 5ml, 1 tbsp = 15ml, 1 cup = 250ml/8fl oz.
Australian standard tablespoons are 20ml. Australian readers should use 3 tsp in place of 1 tbsp for measuring small quantities.
American pints are 16fl oz/2 cups. American readers should use 20fl oz/2.5 cups in place of 1 pint when measuring liquids.
Electric oven temperatures in this book are for conventional ovens. When using a fan oven, the temperature will probably need to be reduced by about 10–20°C/20–40°F. Since ovens vary, you should check with your manufacturer's instruction book for guidance.
The nutritional analysis given for each recipe is calculated per portion (i.e. serving or item), unless otherwise stated. If the recipe gives a range, such as Serves 4–6, then the nutritional analysis will be for the smaller portion size, i.e. 6 servings. Measurements for sodium do not include salt added to taste.
Medium (US large) eggs are used unless otherwise stated.

CONTENTS

INTRODUCTION

The Greeks enjoy the simple things in life: sun, sea and fresh air. They also like to eat well, and after centuries of experimenting, they have developed an exquisite flavour to their food that is recognized and enjoyed throughout the world. The country's geographic setting is such that its cuisine has benefitted from the Orient as well as from Europe, and this has created an array of delicious tastes that are unique. The main ingredients used in Greek cooking are olive oil, herbs, fresh tomatoes and lemons.

Food and drink are at the centre of the social life of the Greeks. They are known to relax and amuse themselves for hours around the table, where eating and drinking provide the inspiration for many a philosophical discussion about life, politics or even football.

While sitting and talking in the Mediterranean sunshine, the Greeks are often seen sipping coffee, or a drink, usually with meze, which is perhaps the most famous feature of their cuisine. A meze is a small portion of something delicious – it can be anything from a

Right: Together with its healthy qualities, olive oil is indispensable to Greek cooking for its fine, nutty flavour.

creamy dip to a plate of elaborately stuffed vegetables, or perhaps even just a few fresh olives. This may also be accompanied by the rhythmic sound of the bazouki, the Greek equivalent to the guitar, which can often be heard late into the night. A meze often also proves to be a convenient way to serve unexpected guests at the table. In villages, a place is always found for a stranger at the table. During such a meal, a guest is likely to be offered a choice of meat or a particular fruit from the host's own plate – such a gesture should not be refused.

One essential feature of Greek cuisine is the use of fresh ingredients. Meat and fish are often simply grilled, and served with fresh herbs and lemon juice, accompanied by a refreshing Greek salad. Such cooking methods have evolved around the abundance of fish, available from the coastlines around mainland Greece and the islands.

Chicken and lamb are the most commonly eaten meats, due to the rather rugged terrain which is unsuited to raising cattle, especially during the long hot summertime. Meat is often cooked in a similar way to fish, on a barbecue or spit. A family's roasting lamb sends out an inviting spicy aroma from one garden to the next.

In rural areas, where many families rely upon the cultivation of land, people tend to eat what is in season. In winter, Avgolemono Soup (made with egg and lemon) is tangy and refreshingly light. In the autumn, black-eye beans served with greens is a popular dish, or chicken with pilafi (rice cooked in the juice of the meat). Horta is extremely popular, a wild green not unlike spinach in taste and equally strong in iron content. Okra is also a favourite vegetable. A common addition to the Greek table is an alcoholic drink, which is an important part of the enjoyment of food. Indeed, Greeks regard all people who drink without eating as not quite civilized. Perhaps the most famous drink is ouzo, an aniseed tasting spirit that turns cloudy when water is added.

Left: Greece, in south-east Europe, occupies the southern part of the Balkan Peninsula and many islands in the Ionian and Aegean Seas.

EUROPE

BLACK SEA

THRACE

MACEDONIA

Thessaloniki

SEA OF MARMARA

Thassos

Samothraki

EPIRUS

Corfu

THESSALY

Limnos

AEGEAN SEA

Sporades

Lesvos

ASIA

Keffallinia

ATTICA

Chios

Athens

Zakynthos

PELOPONNESE

Andros

Samos

Ikaria

IONIAN SEA

Cyclades

Kos

Dodecanese

Thira

Rhodes

Kythira

Karpathos

Herakleion

CRETE

MEDITERRANEAN SEA

Above: In Greece, sweet peppers are served stuffed, filled with couscous, rice, herbs, spices, dried fruits, nuts, cheese and sometimes meat.

Breakfast is simply coffee, similar to Turkish coffee, and perhaps a slice of bread or a few biscuits. Lunch starts about two in the afternoon and lasts for an hour or so. The evening meal is taken at around ten o'clock and can last well into the night. Fruit is plentiful according to the season, with an abundance of melons, apricots and peaches and a choice of over three hundred grape varieties. There are also many sweet pastries to choose from, although these are more often seen as a speciality rather than a common dessert.

Above all, the secret of making and enjoying a Greek meal is not to rush it, but rather to sit long over each course in the company of friends and family.

Right: Chickpeas are puréed with olive oil to produce hummus, a delicious and extremely popular dip.

SOUPS AND
MEZEDES

Greek food offers a wonderful array of soups and appetizers.

The Greek word "mezedes" means "a tableful" and it comes from

the tradition of sharing small dishes of savoury foods while relaxing

with cool drinks. You will find a variety of flavours to sample, from

a spicy and warming Pumpkin Soup, to a creamy Aubergine Dip

and tasty Lamb and Potato Cakes.

LENTIL SOUP

PULSES ARE A WINTER STAPLE IN GREECE, LENTILS A PARTICULARLY DELICIOUS VARIETY. AS THEY DO NOT NEED SOAKING, THEY MAKE AN EASY OPTION FOR A QUICK MEAL. THE SECRET OF GOOD LENTIL SOUP IS TO BE GENEROUS WITH THE OLIVE OIL. THE SOUP IS SERVED AS A MAIN MEAL, ACCOMPANIED BY OLIVES, BREAD AND CHEESE OR, FOR A SPECIAL OCCASION, WITH FRIED SQUID OR KEFTEDES.

SERVES FOUR

INGREDIENTS

275g/10oz/1¼ cups brown-green
  lentils, preferably the small variety
150ml/¼ pint/⅔ cup extra virgin
  olive oil
1 onion, thinly sliced
2 garlic cloves, sliced into thin batons
1 carrot, sliced into thin discs
400g/14oz can chopped tomatoes
15ml/1 tbsp tomato purée (paste)
2.5ml/½ tsp dried oregano
1 litre/1¾ pints/4 cups hot water
salt and ground black pepper
30ml/2 tbsp roughly chopped fresh
  herb leaves, to garnish

1 Rinse the brown-green lentils thoroughly, drain them and put them in a large pan with cold water to cover. Bring the water to the boil and boil for 3–4 minutes. Strain, discarding the liquid, and set the lentils aside.

2 Wipe the pan clean and add the extra virgin olive oil. Place it over a medium heat until hot and then add the thinly sliced onion and sauté until translucent. Stir in the sliced garlic, then, as soon as it becomes aromatic, return the lentils to the pan. Add the carrot, tomatoes, tomato purée and oregano. Stir in the hot water and a little ground black pepper to taste.

3 Bring the soup to the boil, then lower the heat, cover the pan and cook gently for 20–30 minutes, until the lentils feel soft but have not begun to disintegrate. Add salt and the chopped herbs just before serving.

Energy 462Kcal/1,935kJ; Protein 18.4g; Carbohydrate 40g, of which sugars 6.6g; Fat 26.6g, of which saturates 3.7g; Cholesterol 0mg; Calcium 86mg; Fibre 8g; Sodium 64mg.

CHICKPEA SOUP

This traditional Greek winter staple is enjoyable in any season, even during the hot summer months. Compared to other soups based on pulses, which are often very hearty, this has a unique lightness in terms of both flavour and texture. It can be enjoyed as an appetizer, or can be a delicious healthy main meal with fresh bread and feta cheese.

SERVES FOUR

INGREDIENTS
  150ml/¼ pint/⅔ cup extra virgin
    olive oil, plus extra for drizzling
    and serving
  1 large onion, chopped
  350g/12oz/1¾ cups dried
    chickpeas, soaked in cold water
    overnight
  15ml/1 tbsp plain
    (all-purpose) flour
  juice of 1 lemon, or to taste
  45ml/3 tbsp chopped fresh flat
    leaf parsley
  salt and ground black pepper

1 Heat the extra virgin olive oil in a heavy pan, add the onion and sauté until it starts to colour.

2 Meanwhile, drain the chickpeas, rinse them under cold water and drain them again. Shake the colander or sieve to dry the chickpeas as much as possible, then add them to the pan. Turn them with a spatula for a few minutes to coat them well in the oil, then pour in enough hot water to cover them by about 4cm/1½in.

3 Slowly bring to the boil. Skim off any white froth that rises to the surface, using a slotted spoon, and discard. Lower the heat to achieve a simmer, add some freshly ground black pepper, cover and cook for 1–1¼ hours, or until the chickpeas are soft.

4 Put the flour in a cup and stir in the lemon juice with a fork. When the chickpeas are perfectly soft, add this mixture to them. Mix well, then add salt and pepper to taste. Cover the pan and cook gently for 5–10 minutes more, stirring occasionally.

5 To thicken the soup slightly, take out about two cupfuls of the chickpeas and put them in a food processor or blender. Process briefly so that the chickpeas are broken up, but remain slightly rough. Stir into the soup in the pan and mix well.

6 Add the parsley, then taste the soup and add more lemon juice if bland. Serve in heated bowls and offer extra olive oil at the table, for drizzling.

Energy 544Kcal/2,274kJ; Protein 20.1g; Carbohydrate 51.6g, of which sugars 6.1g; Fat 30g, of which saturates 4g; Cholesterol 0mg; Calcium 184mg; Fibre 10.9g; Sodium 40mg.

AVGOLEMONO

THIS IS A GREAT FAVOURITE IN GREECE AND IS A FINE EXAMPLE OF HOW A FEW INGREDIENTS CAN MAKE A MARVELLOUS DISH IF CAREFULLY CHOSEN AND COOKED. IT IS ESSENTIAL TO USE A WELL-FLAVOURED STOCK. ADD AS LITTLE OR AS MUCH RICE AS YOU LIKE.

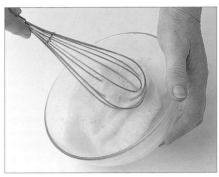

2 Whisk the egg yolks in a bowl, then add about 30ml/2 tbsp of the lemon juice, whisking constantly until the mixture is smooth and bubbly. Add a ladleful of soup and whisk again.

3 Remove the soup from the heat and slowly add the egg mixture, whisking all the time. The soup will turn a pretty lemon colour and will thicken slightly.

4 Taste and add more lemon juice if necessary. Stir in the parsley. Serve at once, without reheating, garnished with lemon slices and parsley sprigs.

SERVES 4

INGREDIENTS
  900ml/1½ pints/3¾ cups chicken
    stock, preferably home-made
  50g/2oz/generous ⅓ cup long
    grain rice
  3 egg yolks
  30–60ml/2–4 tbsp lemon juice
  30ml/2 tbsp finely chopped fresh
    parsley
  salt and freshly ground black pepper
  lemon slices and parsley sprigs,
    to garnish

1 Pour the stock into a pan, bring to simmering point, then add the drained rice. Half cover and cook for about 12 minutes until the rice is just tender. Season with salt and pepper.

COOK'S TIP
The trick here is to add the egg mixture to the soup without it curdling. Avoid whisking the mixture into boiling liquid. It is safest to remove the soup from the heat entirely and then whisk in the mixture in a slow but steady stream. Do not reheat as curdling would be almost inevitable.

Energy 96Kcal/404kJ; Protein 3.3g; Carbohydrate 10.9g, of which sugars 0.2g; Fat 4.7g, of which saturates 1.2g; Cholesterol 151mg; Calcium 39mg; Fibre 0.4g; Sodium 10mg.

Spicy Pumpkin Soup

Pumpkin is popular all over Greece and it's an important ingredient in Middle-Eastern cooking, from which this soup is inspired. Ginger and cumin give the soup its wonderful spicy flavour, making it a hearty and flavoursome meal.

SERVES FOUR

INGREDIENTS
  900g/2lb pumpkin, peeled and
    seeds removed
  30ml/2 tbsp extra virgin olive oil
  2 leeks, trimmed and sliced
  1 garlic clove, crushed
  5ml/1 tsp ground ginger
  5ml/1 tsp ground cumin
  900ml/1½ pints/3¾ cups
    chicken stock
  salt and ground black pepper
  coriander (cilantro) leaves, to garnish
  60ml/4 tbsp Greek (US strained
    plain) yogurt, to serve

1 Cut the pumpkin flesh into evenly sized chunks. Heat the oil in a large pan and add the leeks and garlic. Cook gently until softened.

2 Add the ground ginger and cumin and cook, stirring, for a further minute. Add the pumpkin chunks and the chicken stock and season with salt and pepper. Bring the mixture to the boil and simmer for 30 minutes, or until the pumpkin is tender. Process the soup, in batches if necessary, in a blender or food processor.

3 Reheat the soup gently, and ladle out into four warmed individual bowls. Add a spoon of Greek yogurt on the top of each and swirl it through the top layer of soup. Garnish with chopped fresh coriander leaves.

Energy 98Kcal/409kJ; Protein 3g; Carbohydrate 7.5g, of which sugars 5.8g; Fat 6.4g, of which saturates 1.1g; Cholesterol 0mg; Calcium 86mg; Fibre 4.2g; Sodium 2mg.

TARAMASALATA

*THIS DELICIOUS SPECIALITY MAKES AN EXCELLENT START TO ANY MEAL. IT IS PERHAPS ONE OF THE
MOST FAMOUS GREEK DIPS, AND A CENTRAL PART OF ANY MEZE TABLE.*

SERVES FOUR

INGREDIENTS
115g/4oz smoked mullet roe
2 garlic cloves, crushed
30ml/2 tbsp grated onion
60ml/4 tbsp olive oil
4 slices white bread,
 crusts removed
juice of 2 lemons
30ml/2 tbsp milk or water
freshly ground black pepper
warm pitta bread, to serve

COOK'S TIP
Since the roe of grey mullet is expensive,
smoked cod's roe is often used instead
for this dish. It is paler than the burnt
orange colour of mullet roe but is still
very good.

1 Place the smoked fish roe, garlic,
grated onion, oil, bread and lemon juice
in a blender or food processor and
process until smooth.

2 Scrape down the edges of the food
processor or blender to ensure that
all the ingredients are properly
incorporated. Blend quickly again.

3 Add the milk or water and process
again for a few seconds. (This will give
the *taramasalata* a creamier texture.)

4 Pour the *taramasalata* into a serving
bowl, cover with clear film (plastic wrap)
and chill for 1–2 hours before serving.
Sprinkle the dip with black pepper and
serve with warm pitta bread.

Energy 185Kcal/770kJ; Protein 8.4g; Carbohydrate 11.4g, of which sugars 1.7g; Fat 12.1g, of which saturates 1.8g; Cholesterol 95mg; Calcium 38mg; Fibre 0.5g; Sodium 139mg.

FETA <u>AND</u> ROAST PEPPER DIP <u>WITH</u> CHILLIES

THIS IS A FAMILIAR MEZE IN THE BEAUTIFUL CITY OF THESSALONIKA. IF YOU STOP FOR AN OUZO IN THE AREA CALLED LATHATHIKA YOU WILL INEVITABLY BE SERVED A SMALL PLATE OF HTIPITI.

SERVES FOUR

INGREDIENTS

1 yellow or green elongated or
   bell-shaped pepper
1–2 fresh green chillies
200g/7oz feta cheese, cubed
60ml/4 tbsp extra virgin
   olive oil
juice of 1 lemon
45–60ml/3–4 tbsp milk
ground black pepper
finely chopped fresh flat leaf parsley,
   to garnish
slices of toast or toasted pitta bread,
   to serve

VARIATION

The dip is also excellent served with a selection of vegetable crudités, such as carrot, cauliflower, green or red (bell) pepper and celery.

1 Scorch the pepper and chillies by threading them on to metal skewers and turning them over a flame or under the grill (broiler), until charred all over.

2 Set the pepper and chillies aside until cool enough to handle. Peel off as much of their skin as possible and wipe off the blackened parts with kitchen paper. Slit the pepper and chillies and discard the seeds and stems.

3 Put the pepper and chilli flesh into a food processor. Add the feta cheese, olive oil, lemon juice and milk, and blend well. Add a little more milk if the mixture is too stiff, and season with black pepper. Spread the dip on slices of toast, sprinkle a little fresh parsley over the top and serve.

Energy 245Kcal/1,014kJ; Protein 8.7g; Carbohydrate 4.5g, of which sugars 4.3g; Fat 21.5g, of which saturates 8.6g; Cholesterol 36mg; Calcium 198mg; Fibre 0.8g; Sodium 727mg.

AUBERGINE DIP

ADJUST THE AMOUNT OF AUBERGINE, GARLIC AND LEMON JUICE IN THIS RICHLY FLAVOURED AUBERGINE DIP DEPENDING ON HOW CREAMY, GARLICKY OR TART YOU WANT IT TO BE. THE DIP CAN BE SERVED WITH A GARNISH OF CHOPPED FRESH CORIANDER LEAVES, OLIVES OR PICKLED CUCUMBERS. HOT PEPPER SAUCE OR A LITTLE GROUND CORIANDER CAN BE ADDED, TOO.

SERVES TWO TO FOUR

INGREDIENTS
    1 large or 2 medium aubergines
      (eggplants)
    2–4 garlic cloves, chopped
    90–150ml/6–10 tbsp tahini
    juice of 1 lemon, or to taste
    salt and ground black pepper

COOK'S TIPS
You can grill or broil the aubergines instead of cooking them directly over a flame. Brush each side very lightly with extra virgin olive oil and then place under a hot grill (broiler), turning frequently, until charred all around.

1 Place the aubergine(s) directly over the flame of a gas stove or on the coals of a barbecue. Turn the aubergine(s) fairly frequently until deflated and the skin is evenly charred. Remove from the heat with tongs.

2 Put the aubergine(s) in a plastic bag and seal the top tightly, or place in a bowl and cover with plenty of sheets of crumpled kitchen paper. Leave to cool for 30–60 minutes.

3 Peel off the blackened skin from the aubergine(s), reserving the juices. Chop the aubergine flesh, either by hand for a coarse texture or in a food processor or blender for a smooth purée. Put the aubergine in a bowl and stir in the reserved juices.

4 Add the chopped garlic and tahini to the aubergine and stir until smooth. You may prefer not to add all of the other ingredients all at once, but keep a little to one side to add after tasting.

5 Stir in the lemon juice. If the mixture becomes too thick, add 15–30ml/ 1–2 tbsp water. Season with salt and freshly ground black pepper to taste and spoon into a serving bowl. Serve at room temperature. Garnish with olives and a few sprigs of fresh coriander (cilantro) or fresh mint.

Energy 303Kcal/1256kJ; Protein 10.3g; Carbohydrate 5g, of which sugars 3.3g; Fat 27.2g, of which saturates 4g; Cholesterol 0mg; Calcium 323mg; Fibre 6.9g; Sodium 13mg.

HUMMUS

THIS CLASSIC GREEK CHICKPEA DIP IS FLAVOURED WITH GARLIC AND TAHINI — SESAME SEED PASTE. FOR EXTRA FLAVOUR, A LITTLE GROUND CUMIN CAN BE ADDED, AND OLIVE OIL CAN ALSO BE STIRRED IN TO ENRICH THE HUMMUS, IF YOU LIKE. IT IS DELICIOUS SERVED WITH WEDGES OF TOASTED PITTA BREAD OR WITH CRUDITÉS AS A DELICIOUS DIP.

SERVES FOUR TO SIX

INGREDIENTS
400g/14oz can chickpeas, drained
60ml/4 tbsp tahini
2–3 garlic cloves, chopped
juice of ½–1 lemon
salt and ground black pepper
whole chickpeas reserved,
  to garnish

VARIATION
Process 2 roasted red (bell) peppers with the chickpeas, then continue as above. Serve sprinkled with lightly toasted pine nuts and paprika mixed with a little extra virgin olive oil.

1 Reserving a few for garnish, coarsely mash the chickpeas in a mixing bowl with a fork. If you like a smoother purée, process the chickpeas in a food processor or blender until a smooth paste is formed.

2 Mix the tahini into the bowl of chickpeas, then stir in the chopped garlic cloves and lemon juice. Season to taste and garnish the top with the reserved chickpeas. Serve the hummus at room temperature.

Energy 210Kcal/880kJ; Protein 10.3g; Carbohydrate 16.9g, of which sugars 0.6g; Fat 11.8g, of which saturates 1.6g; Cholesterol 0mg; Calcium 146mg; Fibre 5.5g; Sodium 223mg.

LAMB AND POTATO CAKES

AN UNUSUAL DISH, THESE MINCED LAMB TRIANGLES ARE EASY TO SERVE HOT FOR A BUFFET, OR THEY CAN BE EATEN COLD AS A SNACK. THEY ARE ALSO EXCELLENT FOR PICNICS.

MAKES TWELVE TO FIFTEEN

INGREDIENTS
450g/1lb new or small,
  firm potatoes
3 eggs
1 onion, grated
30ml/2 tbsp chopped fresh
  flat leaf parsley
450g/1lb/2 cups finely minced
  (ground) lean lamb
115g/4oz/2 cups fresh
  breadcrumbs
vegetable oil, for frying
salt and ground black pepper
a few sprigs of fresh mint,
  to garnish
toasted pitta bread and herby green
  salad, to serve

1 Cook the potatoes in a large pan of boiling salted water for 20 minutes, or until tender, then drain and leave to one side to cool.

2 Beat the eggs in a large bowl. Add the grated onion, parsley and seasoning and beat together.

3 When the potatoes are cold, grate them coarsely and stir into the egg mixture. Then add the minced lamb and stir in, using your hands to blend the mixture fully. Knead for 3–4 minutes, or until the ingredients are thoroughly blended.

4 Take a handful of the lamb and potato mixture and roll it into a ball, about the size of a golf ball. Repeat this process until all is used.

5 Roll the balls in the breadcrumbs and then mould them into thin triangular shapes, about 13cm/5in long. Coat them in the breadcrumbs again on both sides.

6 Heat a 1cm/½in layer of oil in a frying pan over a medium heat. When the oil is hot, fry the potato cakes for 8–12 minutes, or until golden brown on both sides, turning occasionally. Drain well on a plate covered with a few layers of kitchen paper, changing the paper when necessary. Serve hot, garnished with a few sprigs of fresh mint and accompanied by freshly toasted pitta bread and a green salad.

Energy 181Kcal/760kJ; Protein 10.8g; Carbohydrate 13.9g, of which sugars 1.1g; Fat 9.6g, of which saturates 2.8g; Cholesterol 76mg; Calcium 31mg; Fibre 0.8g; Sodium 128mg.

COURGETTE RISSOLES <u>FROM</u> ALONNISOS

THESE TASTY KOLOKYTHOKEFTEES *ARE AN INGENIOUS WAY OF TRANSFORMING BLAND-TASTING COURGETTES INTO A SHARPLY APPETIZING DISH THAT CAPTIVATES EVERYONE WHO TRIES IT.*

SERVES SIX

INGREDIENTS
    500g/1¼lb courgettes (zucchini)
    120ml/4fl oz/½ cup extra virgin
        olive oil
    1 large onion, finely chopped
    2 spring onions (scallions), green and
        white parts finely chopped
    1 garlic clove, crushed
    3 medium slices of bread (not from a
        pre-sliced loaf)
    2 eggs, lightly beaten
    200g/7oz feta cheese, crumbled
    50g/2oz/½ cup freshly grated Greek
        Graviera or Italian Parmesan cheese
    45–60ml/3–4 tbsp finely chopped
        fresh dill or 5ml/1 tsp dried oregano
    50g/2oz/½ cup plain
        (all-purpose) flour
    salt and ground black pepper
    6 lemon wedges, to serve

1 Bring a pan of lightly salted water to the boil. Slice the courgettes into 4cm/1½in lengths and place them in the boiling water. Cover and cook for about 10 minutes. Drain in a colander and let them cool completely.

2 Heat 45ml/3 tbsp of the olive oil in a frying pan, add the onion and spring onions and sauté until translucent. Add the garlic, then, as soon as it becomes aromatic, take the pan off the heat.

3 Squeeze the courgettes with your hands, to extract as much water as possible, then place them in a large bowl. Add the fried onion and garlic mixture and mix well.

4 Toast the bread, cut off and discard the crusts, then break up the toast and crumb it in a food processor. Add the crumbs to the courgette mixture, with the eggs, feta cheese and grated Graviera or Parmesan.

5 Stir the dill or oregano into the courgette mixture, and add salt and pepper to taste. If the mixture seems too wet, add a little flour.

6 Take a heaped tablespoon of the courgette mixture, roll it into a round ball, using your hands, and press it lightly to make a rissole shape. Make more rissoles in the same way.

7 Coat the rissoles lightly in the flour. Heat the remaining extra virgin olive oil in a large, non-stick frying pan, then fry the rissoles in batches until they are crisp and brown, turning them over once. Drain on kitchen paper and serve with the lemon wedges.

Energy 343Kcal/1,424kJ; Protein 14.7g; Carbohydrate 18.5g, of which sugars 4.9g; Fat 23.9g, of which saturates 8.6g; Cholesterol 95mg; Calcium 301mg; Fibre 2.2g; Sodium 668mg.

DEEP-FRIED WHITEBAIT

IN GREECE THE SMALLEST FISH OF THE CATCH ARE ALWAYS FRIED. HERE, FISH ARE LIGHTLY FLOURED IN A SPICY MIXTURE AND FRIED INDIVIDUALLY TO MAKE THE FAVOURITE DISH, MARIDES.

SERVES FOUR

INGREDIENTS
    115g/4oz/1 cup plain
      (all-purpose) flour
    2.5ml/½ tsp paprika
    2.5ml/½ tsp ground cayenne pepper
    1.1kg/2½lb whitebait
    vegetable oil, for deep frying
    lemon wedges, to serve

1 Put the flour in a large bowl and mix in the paprika, cayenne pepper and salt.

2 Add the whitebait to the bowl in batches and coat evenly with the flour. If you are using frozen whitebait, ensure that it is properly thawed before preparation.

3 Heat the vegetable oil in a large, heavy pan over a medium to high heat until it reaches a temperature of 190°C/375°F. Fry the whitebait in batches of about a dozen in a mesh basket for 2 minutes, or until the fish is golden and crispy.

4 Drain the fried fish well on a plate covered with absorbent kitchen paper and serve hot with lemon wedges. Whitebait are often served with dips, such as Greek yogurt dips, mayonnaise, cocktail or tartar sauce.

COOK'S TIP
Whitebait are not one species of fish, as is often thought, but a mixture of the fry of sprats, herrings and other small fish. There can be as many as 20 different fish in one catch.

Energy 1,444Kcal/5,979kJ; Protein 53.6g; Carbohydrate 14.6g, of which sugars 0.3g; Fat 130.6g, of which saturates 12.1g; Cholesterol 0mg; Calcium 2,365mg; Fibre 0.6g; Sodium 633mg.

OCTOPUS SALAD

IN THE COASTAL AREAS OF MAINLAND GREECE AND ON THE ISLANDS, OCTOPUS IS A PARTICULAR FAVOURITE, AND MAKES A DELICIOUS SALAD.

SERVES FOUR TO SIX

INGREDIENTS

    900g/2lb baby octopus or squid, skinned
    175ml/6fl oz/¾ cup olive oil
    30ml/2 tbsp white wine vinegar
    30ml/2 tbsp chopped fresh parsley or coriander (cilantro)
    12 black olives, stoned (pitted)
    2 shallots, thinly sliced
    1 red onion, thinly sliced
    salt and ground black pepper
    sprigs of coriander, to garnish
    8–12 cos or romaine lettuce leaves and lemon wedges, to serve

1 In a large pan, boil the octopus or squid in salted water for 20–25 minutes, or until just soft. Drain and leave to cool completely before covering and chilling for 45 minutes.

2 Spread out the octopus on a large chopping board. Cut the tentacles from the body and head, then chop all the flesh into even pieces, slicing across the thick part of the tentacles and following the direction of the suckers. If using squid, chop into even rings.

3 In a bowl, combine the olive oil and white wine vinegar.

COOK'S TIP
Take care not to overcook the octopus or squid or it will become tough and rubbery.

4 Add the herbs, olives, shallots, octopus and red onion to the bowl. Season to taste and toss well.

5 Arrange the octopus on a bed of lettuce, garnish with coriander and serve with lemon wedges.

Energy 481Kcal/2,001kJ; Protein 35.2g; Carbohydrate 4.3g, of which sugars 1.2g; Fat 36.1g, of which saturates 5.5g; Cholesterol 506mg; Calcium 56mg; Fibre 0.9g; Sodium 420mg.

FISH AND SHELLFISH

  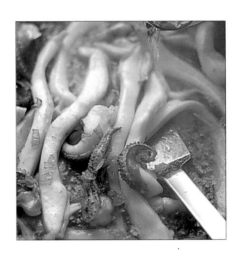

Because Greece is a peninsula with many islands, fish and shellfish are widely available and enjoyed super-fresh from the sea. Although fish is often simply grilled, fried or barbecued, many dishes include rich sauces or are flavoured with combinations of herbs, citrus fruits, spices and vegetables. There are some exciting dishes to be had — try a tempting Fish Plaki, tangy Baked Red Mullet with Oranges, or Baked Fish with Tahini Sauce.

SQUID WITH SPINACH

THIS IS AN UNUSUAL DISH, WHICH IS OCCASIONALLY MADE FOR SPECIAL FEASTS ON THE ISLAND OF CRETE. SQUID IS A WONDERFUL INGREDIENT, ESPECIALLY WHEN IT IS USED FRESH. THIS DISH MAKES A SUPERB MEAL WITH CRUSTY BREAD AND CRISP, FRESH SALAD.

SERVES FOUR

INGREDIENTS

  1kg/2¼lb fresh squid, cleaned
  120ml/4fl oz/½ cup extra virgin
    olive oil
  1 large onion, sliced
  3 spring onions (scallions), chopped
  175ml/6fl oz/¾ cup white wine
  150ml/¼ pint/⅔ cup hot water
  500g/1¼lb fresh spinach
  juice of ½ lemon
  45ml/3 tbsp chopped fresh dill
  salt and ground black pepper
  chunks of fresh white bread,
    to serve

1 Rinse the squid thoroughly inside and out, and drain well. Slice the body in half vertically, then slice into 1cm/½in strips. Cut each tentacle into smaller pieces.

2 Heat the oil in a wide, heavy pan and sauté the onion slices and spring onions gently until the onion slices are translucent.

COOK'S TIP
When buying squid, try to buy the smaller ones as they are generally more tender than larger squid. The wine in this recipe also helps to tenderize the flesh.

3 Increase the heat and add the slices of squid, including the smaller pieces of tentacles. The process will produce some moisture, but keep stirring and this will evaporate. Continue to stir for 10 minutes more, or until the squid starts to turn golden.

4 Pour in the wine and stir in, letting it evaporate slightly. Then add the hot water, with salt and freshly ground black pepper to taste. The flavour will change after further cooking so do not add too much seasoning at this stage. Cover the pan and cook for about 30 minutes, stirring occasionally.

5 Wash the spinach well and drain it carefully, removing any excess moisture with kitchen paper. Remove any stalks and chop it coarsely. Stir into the pan.

6 When the chopped spinach starts to wilt, cover the pan and cook for about 10 minutes. Just before serving, add the lemon juice and dill and mix well. Serve this dish in shallow bowls or on plates with fresh bread. Accompany with a fresh side salad.

Energy 462Kcal/1,931kJ; Protein 42.8g; Carbohydrate 9.5g, of which sugars 5.2g; Fat 25.4g, of which saturates 4g; Cholesterol 563mg; Calcium 264mg; Fibre 3.5g; Sodium 454mg.

OCTOPUS AND PASTA BAKE

A MOUTHWATERING DISH, THIS SLOW-COOKED COMBINATION OF OCTOPUS AND PASTA IN A SPICY TOMATO SAUCE IS QUITE AN EVERYDAY AFFAIR IN GREECE, ESPECIALLY ON THE ISLANDS WHERE OCTOPUS ARE READILY AVAILABLE FROM MARKETS AND AT THE HARBOURS.

SERVES FOUR

INGREDIENTS

2 octopuses, total weight about
    675–800g/1½–1¾lb, cleaned
150ml/¼ pint/⅔ cup extra virgin
    olive oil
2 large onions, sliced
3 garlic cloves, chopped
1 fresh red or green chilli, seeded
    and thinly sliced
1 or 2 bay leaves
5ml/1 tsp dried oregano
1 piece of cinnamon stick
2 or 3 grains allspice (optional)
175ml/6fl oz/¾ cup red wine
30ml/2 tbsp tomato purée (paste)
    diluted in 300ml/½ pint/1¼ cups
    warm water
300ml/½ pint/1¼ cups
    boiling water
225g/8oz/2 cups dried penne or
    small macaroni-type pasta
ground black pepper
45ml/3 tbsp finely chopped
    fresh flat leaf parsley, to garnish
    (optional)

1 Rinse the octopuses well, making sure that there is no sand left in the suckers. Cut the octopuses into large cubes using a sharp knife and place the pieces in a heavy pan over a low heat. Cook gently; they will produce some liquid, the colour of the flesh will change and they will eventually become bright scarlet. Keep turning the pieces of octopus with a wooden spatula until all the liquid has evaporated.

2 Add the olive oil to the pan and sauté the octopus pieces for 4–5 minutes. Add the sliced onions to the pan and cook for a further 4–5 minutes, stirring them constantly until they start to turn golden.

3 Stir in the chopped garlic, chilli, bay leaf or leaves, oregano, cinnamon stick and allspice, if using. As soon as the garlic becomes aromatic, pour in the wine and let it bubble and evaporate for a couple of minutes.

4 Pour in the diluted tomato purée, add some black pepper, cover and cook gently for 1½ hours, or until the octopus is perfectly soft. Stir occasionally and add a little hot water if needed. The dish can be prepared up to this stage well in advance of serving.

5 Preheat the oven to 160°C/325°F/ Gas 3. Bring the octopus mixture to the boil, and then add the boiling water, stirring it into the mixture.

6 Stir in the dried pasta, coating it in the mixture. Tip the mixture into a large roasting dish and level the surface. Transfer to the oven and bake for 30–35 minutes, stirring occasionally and adding a little hot water if the mixture starts to look dry. Sprinkle the parsley on top, if using, and serve.

COOK'S TIPS
• Do not add salt to octopus as it makes it tough and indigestible.
• The octopus mixture can be cooked in a pressure cooker, if you prefer. It will take 20 minutes under full pressure.

Energy 637Kcal/2,669kJ; Protein 38.9g; Carbohydrate 52.9g, of which sugars 10.2g; Fat 28.5g, of which saturates 4.2g; Cholesterol 81mg; Calcium 108mg; Fibre 3.6g; Sodium 25mg.

CUTTLEFISH WITH POTATOES

SAUTÉED CUTTLEFISH IS SWEETER AND MORE TENDER THAN SQUID, PROVIDED YOU BUY SMALL OR MEDIUM-SIZE SPECIMENS. SERVE AS A SUMPTUOUS MAIN COURSE OR A TASTY MEZE DISH.

SERVES FOUR AS A MAIN COURSE,
SIX AS A FIRST COURSE

INGREDIENTS
  1kg/2¼lb fresh cuttlefish,
    cleaned
  150ml/¼ pint/⅔ cup extra virgin
    olive oil
  1 large onion, about 225g/8oz,
    chopped
  175ml/6fl oz/¾ cup
    white wine
  300ml/½ pint/1¼ cups
    hot water
  500g/1¼lb potatoes, peeled
    and cubed
  4–5 spring onions (scallions),
    chopped
  juice of 1 lemon
  60ml/4 tbsp chopped
    fresh dill
  salt and ground black pepper

1 Rinse and drain the cleaned cuttlefish well, then slice them into 2cm/¾in wide ribbons.

2 Heat the oil in a heavy pan, add the onion and sauté for about 5 minutes until light golden. Add the cuttlefish and sauté until all the water they exude has evaporated and the flesh starts to change colour. This will take 10–15 minutes.

3 Pour in the wine and, when it has evaporated, add the water. Cover and cook for 10 minutes.

4 Add the potatoes, spring onions, lemon juice, and salt and pepper. There should be enough water almost to cover the ingredients; top up if necessary. Cover and cook gently for 40 minutes, or until the cuttlefish is tender. Add the dill and cook for 5 minutes. Serve hot.

Energy 540Kcal/2,254kJ; Protein 43.3g; Carbohydrate 24.7g, of which sugars 5.1g; Fat 27.3g, of which saturates 4.2g; Cholesterol 275mg; Calcium 176mg; Fibre 2.2g; Sodium 943mg.

GRILLED KING PRAWNS WITH PIQUANT SAUCE

THIS WELL-FLAVOURED SAUCE IS SERVED WITH FISH AND SHELLFISH. THE SWEET PEPPER, TOMATOES,
GARLIC, CHILLI AND TOASTED ALMONDS GO EXCEEDINGLY WELL WITH ROBUST PRAWNS.

SERVES FOUR

INGREDIENTS
  24 raw king prawns (jumbo shrimp)
  30–45ml/2–3 tbsp olive oil
  fresh flat leaf parsley, to garnish
  lemon wedges, to serve

For the sauce
  2 well-flavoured tomatoes
  60ml/4 tbsp olive oil
  1 onion, chopped
  4 garlic cloves, chopped
  1 canned pimiento, chopped
  2.5ml/½ tsp dried chilli flakes
  75ml/5 tbsp fish stock
  30ml/2 tbsp white wine
  10 blanched almonds
  15ml/1 tbsp red wine vinegar
  salt

1 For the sauce, immerse the tomatoes in boiling water for 30 seconds. Peel away the skins and chop the flesh.

2 Heat 30ml/2 tbsp of the oil in a pan, add the onion and 3 of the garlic cloves and cook until soft. Add the pimiento, tomatoes, chilli, fish stock and wine, then cover and simmer for 30 minutes.

3 Spread the whole almonds on a baking sheet and toast them under the grill (broiler) until they are golden-brown. Transfer them to a blender or food processor and grind coarsely. Add the remaining 30ml/2 tbsp of olive oil, the vinegar and the last garlic clove and process until evenly combined. Add the tomato and pimiento sauce and process until smooth and well combined. Season with salt.

4 Remove the heads from the prawns leaving them otherwise unshelled and, with a sharp knife, slit each one down the back and remove the dark vein. Rinse and pat dry on kitchen paper. Preheat the grill. Toss the prawns in olive oil, then spread out in the grill pan. Grill (broil) for about 2–3 minutes on each side, until pink. Arrange on a platter with lemon wedges and the sauce in a small bowl.

Energy 265Kcal/1,097kJ; Protein 12.9g; Carbohydrate 4.7g, of which sugars 3.6g; Fat 21.2g, of which saturates 2.8g; Cholesterol 117mg; Calcium 78mg; Fibre 1.5g; Sodium 120mg.

FISH PLAKI

THE DIFFERENT AREAS OF GREECE AND THE GREEK ISLANDS HAVE A SLIGHTLY DISTINCT VERSION OF THIS SIMPLE BUT VERY DELICIOUS DISH, WHICH MAKES THE MOST OF THE LOCAL FRESH FISH.

SERVES FOUR

INGREDIENTS

    150ml/¼ pint/⅔ cup olive oil
    2 large Spanish onions, chopped
    2 celery sticks, chopped
    4 fat garlic cloves, chopped
    4 potatoes, peeled and diced
    4 carrots, cut into small dice
    15ml/1 tbsp caster (superfine) sugar
    2 bay leaves
    1 thick middle-cut fillet of grouper or
      cod, about 1kg/2¼lb
    16–20 large black olives (optional)
    4 large ripe tomatoes, peeled, seeded
      and chopped
    150ml/¼ pint/⅔ cup dry white wine
      or vermouth
    salt and ground black pepper
    herb leaves, to garnish
    saffron rice, to serve

1 Preheat the oven to 190°C/375°F/ Gas 5. Heat the olive oil in a large frying pan, add the chopped onions and celery and sauté until they are transparent. Add the garlic and cook for 2 minutes more. Stir in the potatoes and carrots and fry for about 5 minutes, stirring occasionally. Sprinkle with the sugar and season to taste with salt and freshly ground black pepper.

2 Grease a large oval or rectangular baking dish, slightly larger than the fish. Spoon the vegetable mixture into the dish, and tuck in the bay leaves.

3 Season the fish and lay it on the bed of vegetables, skin-side up. Sprinkle the olives evenly around the edge, if you are using them.

4 Spread the chopped tomatoes over the fish, pour over the wine or vermouth and season with salt and freshly ground black pepper.

5 Bake for 30–40 minutes, until the fish is cooked through. The type of fish that you are using and the thickness of the fillet may affect the cooking time, so be sure to test the thickest part of the fish to ensure that it is cooked right through. If you are using a whole fish, the cooking time will probably be longer.

6 Serve straight from the dish, garnished with herb leaves, such as fresh dill, chives and flat leaf parsley. Saffron rice would be the ideal accompaniment for the *plaki*.

COOK'S TIP
A whole fish can be used instead of a large fillet, if you prefer.If you use a whole fish, be sure to season it inside as well as out. It can also add flavour to place a bay leaf and sprinkle some of the herbs into the fish as well as over the top. The cooking time will probably be longer with a whole fish so be sure to check the thickest part of the fish before taking it out of the oven.

Energy 557Kcal/2,322kJ; Protein 48.8g; Carbohydrate 24.3g, of which sugars 10.2g; Fat 27.3g, of which saturates 3.9g; Cholesterol 115mg; Calcium 74mg; Fibre 3.3g; Sodium 179mg.

BAKED SALT COD WITH POTATOES AND OLIVES

SALT COD HAS BEEN A WINTER STAPLE IN GREECE FOR GENERATIONS. IT IS ALSO POPULAR DURING THE PERIOD OF LENT, AND IS OFTEN ON THE MENU AT RESTAURANTS ON FRIDAYS DURING THIS TIME.

SERVES FOUR

INGREDIENTS
675g/1½lb salt cod
800g/1¾lb potatoes, cut into wedges
1 large onion, finely chopped
2 or 3 garlic cloves, chopped
leaves from 1 fresh rosemary sprig
30ml/2 tbsp chopped fresh parsley
120ml/4fl oz/½ cup olive oil
400g/14oz can chopped tomatoes
15ml/1 tbsp tomato purée (paste)
300ml/½ pint/1¼ cups hot water
5ml/1 tsp dried oregano
12 black olives
ground black pepper

1 Soak the cod in cold water overnight, changing the water as often as possible in the course of the evening and during the following morning. The cod does not have to be skinned for this dish, but you may prefer to remove the skin, especially if there is a lot of skin on the fish. You should remove any obvious fins or bones. After soaking, drain the cod and cut it into 7cm/2¾in squares.

2 Preheat the oven to 180°C/350°F/ Gas 4. Mix the potatoes, onion, garlic, rosemary and parsley in a large roasting pan with plenty of black pepper. Add the olive oil and toss until coated.

3 Arrange the pieces of cod between the coated vegetables and spread the tomatoes over the surface. Stir the tomato purée into the hot water until dissolved, then pour the mixture over the contents of the pan. Sprinkle the oregano on top. Bake for 1 hour, basting the fish and potatoes occasionally with the pan juices.

4 Remove the roasting pan from the oven, sprinkle the olives on top, and then cook for 30 minutes more, adding a little more hot water if the mixture seems to be drying out. Garnish with fresh parsley. Serve hot or cold.

COOK'S TIP
Salt cod can often be bought from Italian and Spanish groceries, as well as from Greek food stores. It is often sold in small squares, ready for soaking and draining. If you buy it in one piece, cut it into 7cm/2¾in squares; it will shrink slightly with cooking so it is rarely used in smaller pieces than this. Larger chunks may take longer to cook.

Energy 624Kcal/2,624kJ; Protein 61g; Carbohydrate 45.6g, of which sugars 12.9g; Fat 23.3g, of which saturates 3.5g; Cholesterol 100mg; Calcium 98mg; Fibre 4.8g; Sodium 918mg.

GRILLED SWORDFISH SKEWERS

IN GREECE, SEA-FRESH SWORDFISH, OFTEN ON SALE AT THE LOCAL FISH MARKET, IS PERFECT FOR MAKING SOUVLAKI — *SKEWERED AND GRILLED SWORDFISH WITH GARLIC AND OREGANO.*

3 Whisk the olive oil, crushed garlic and oregano in a bowl. Add salt and pepper, and whisk again. Brush the *souvlakia* generously on all sides with the basting sauce.

4 Preheat the grill to the highest setting, or prepare a barbecue. Slide the grill pan or roasting tray underneath the grill or transfer the skewers to the barbecue, making sure that they are not too close to the heat and that the heat is evenly distributed throughout.

5 Cook for 8–10 minutes, turning the skewers several times, until the fish is cooked and the peppers and onions have begun to scorch around the edges. Every time you turn the skewers, brush them with the basting sauce to increase the flavours.

6 Serve the *souvlakia* immediately, garnished with one or two wedges of lemon. Serve with a salad of cucumber, red onion and fresh olives.

COOK'S TIP
Many fishmongers will prepare the swordfish for you, and cut it into cubes for you too. But if you prefer to do this yourself, or you are buying the swordfish whole, you will need approximately 800g/1¾lb swordfish. The cubes should be fairly big – about 5cm/2in square, as they shrink in size as they are cooking. If you have larger cubes of swordfish, you may need to increase the cooking time slightly to ensure that the fish is completely cooked through. If in doubt, cut a large cube open to check.

SERVES FOUR

INGREDIENTS
  2 red onions, quartered
  2 red or green (bell) peppers,
    quartered and seeded
  20–24 thick cubes of swordfish,
    675–800g/1½–1¾lb in total
  75ml/5 tbsp extra virgin olive oil
  1 garlic clove, crushed
  large pinch of dried oregano
  salt and ground black pepper
  lemon wedges, to garnish

1 Carefully separate the onion quarters in pieces, each composed of two or three layers. Slice each pepper quarter in half widthways, or into thirds if you have very large peppers.

2 Make the *souvlakia* by threading five or six pieces of swordfish on to each of four long metal skewers, alternating with pieces of the pepper and onion. Lay the souvlakia across a grill (broiler) pan or roasting tray and set aside while you make the basting sauce.

Energy 363Kcal/1,511kJ; Protein 32.2g; Carbohydrate 11.5g, of which sugars 9.6g; Fat 21.2g, of which saturates 3.6g; Cholesterol 69mg; Calcium 33mg; Fibre 2.5g; Sodium 225mg.

BAKED RED MULLET <u>WITH</u> ORANGES

THE AROMA OF ORANGE ZEST PERVADES MANY OF THE GREEKS' CLASSIC DISHES AND TEMPTS MANY INTO CAFÉS AND RESTAURANTS ON THE MAINLAND AND THROUGHOUT THE ISLANDS.

SERVES FOUR

INGREDIENTS
  a few sprigs of fresh dill
  4 large red mullet, total weight
    1–1.2kg/2¼–2½lb, gutted
    and cleaned
  2 large oranges, halved
  ½ lemon
  60ml/4 tbsp extra virgin
    olive oil
  30ml/2 tbsp pine nuts
  salt

1 Place some fresh dill in the cavity of each fish and lay them in a baking dish, preferably one that can be taken straight to the table. Make sure that the fish are not packed too close together. Sprinkle more dill around the fish.

2 Set half an orange aside and squeeze the rest, along with the lemon. Mix the citrus juices with the olive oil, then pour the mixture over the fish. Turn the fish over so that they are evenly coated in the marinade, then cover and leave in a cool place to marinate for 1–2 hours, spooning the marinade over the fish occasionally.

3 Preheat the oven to 180°C/350°F/ Gas 4. Slice the reserved half orange into thin rounds, then cut each round into quarters. Cover and set aside.

4 Sprinkle a little salt over each fish. Place two or three of the orange wedges over each fish. Bake for 20 minutes, then remove the dish from the oven, baste the fish with the juices and sprinkle the pine nuts over. Return the dish to the oven and bake for 10–15 minutes more.

5 Test the thickest fish to make sure that it is cooked thoroughly, then remove from the oven. You can transfer the fish to a serving platter, garnished with sprigs of fresh dill, or present them in the baking dish.

Energy 344Kcal/1,434kJ; Protein 30.5g; Carbohydrate 5.4g, of which sugars 5.4g; Fat 22.5g, of which saturates 1.9g; Cholesterol 0mg; Calcium 137mg; Fibre 1.2g; Sodium 153mg.

FISH PARCELS

SEA BASS IS GOOD FOR THIS RECIPE, BUT YOU COULD ALSO USE SMALL WHOLE TROUT OR WHITE FISH FILLET SUCH AS COD OR HADDOCK. SERVE WITH CHUNKS OF GOOD CRUSTY BREAD.

SERVES FOUR

INGREDIENTS

    4 pieces sea bass fillet or 4 whole
      small sea bass, about 450g/1lb
      each
    oil, for brushing
    2 shallots, thinly sliced
    1 garlic clove, chopped
    15ml/1 tbsp capers
    6 sun-dried tomatoes, finely
      chopped
    4 black olives, stoned (pitted) and
      thinly sliced
    grated rind and juice of 1 lemon
    5ml/1 tsp paprika
    salt and ground black pepper
    a few sprigs of fresh parsley,
      to garnish
    crusty bread, to serve

1 Preheat the oven to 200°C/400°F/ Gas 6. Clean the fish, if whole. Cut four large squares of double-thickness foil, large enough to enclose the fish. Brush each square with a little oil.

2 Place a piece of fish in the centre of each piece of foil and season well with salt and freshly ground black pepper.

3 Sprinkle over the shallots, garlic, capers, tomatoes, olives and grated lemon rind. Sprinkle with the lemon juice and paprika.

4 Fold the foil over loosely, sealing the edges. Bake in the preheated oven for 15–20 minutes. Remove the foil and serve garnished with parsley.

Energy 343Kcal/1,441kJ; Protein 63.2g; Carbohydrate 2g, of which sugars 1.6g; Fat 9.1g, of which saturates 1.5g; Cholesterol 260mg; Calcium 433mg; Fibre 0.7g; Sodium 396mg.

BAKED FISH <u>IN THE</u> STYLE <u>OF</u> SPETSES

ALL KINDS OF FISH ARE PREPARED IN THIS WAY ON THE TINY ISLAND OF SPETSES. SERVE WITH A LARGE FRESH SALAD, OR WITH LITTLE BOILED POTATOES AND GARLICKY GREEN BEANS, FOR A SUMMER MEAL.

SERVES FOUR

INGREDIENTS
  4 cod or hake steaks
  2 or 3 sprigs of fresh flat
    leaf parsley
  4 slices white bread, toasted, then
    crumbed in a food processor
  salt and ground black pepper

For the sauce
  75–90ml/5–6 tbsp extra virgin
    olive oil
  175ml/6fl oz/¾ cup white wine
  2 garlic cloves, crushed
  60ml/4 tbsp finely chopped flat
    leaf parsley
  1 fresh red or green chilli, seeded
    and finely chopped
  400g/14oz ripe tomatoes, peeled
    and finely diced

1 Mix all the sauce ingredients in a bowl, and add some salt and pepper. Set the mixture aside.

2 Preheat the oven to 190°C/375°F/ Gas 5. Rinse the fish steaks and pat them dry with kitchen paper. Place the steaks in a single layer in an oiled baking dish and sprinkle over the parsley. Season with salt and pepper.

3 Spoon the sauce over the fish, distributing it evenly over each steak. Then sprinkle over half of the breadcrumbs, again evenly covering each steak. Bake for 10 minutes, then baste with the juices in the dish, trying not to disturb the breadcrumbs. Sprinkle with the remaining breadcrumbs, then bake for a further 10–15 minutes.

VARIATION
If you like, use two whole fish, such as sea bass or grey mullet, total weight about 1kg/2¼lb. Rinse thoroughly inside and out, pat dry, then tuck the parsley sprigs inside. Add the sauce and breadcumbs as above. Bake for 15 minutes, then turn both fish over carefully, and bake for 20–25 minutes more.

Energy 362Kcal/1,510kJ; Protein 31g; Carbohydrate 13.1g, of which sugars 3.7g; Fat 17.9g, of which saturates 2.7g; Cholesterol 36mg; Calcium 49mg; Fibre 1.3g; Sodium 274mg.

BAKED FISH WITH TAHINI SAUCE

THRACE AND THE PELOPONNESE ARE RENOWNED FOR THEIR SESAME SEEDS, WHICH ARE USED TO MAKE THE RICH AND CREAMY PASTE, TAHINI. HERE IT IS USED TO CREATE A FRAGRANT TASTE TO BAKED FISH. HARISSA IS A POPULAR FLAVOURING USED THROUGHOUT MAINLAND GREECE AND THE GREEK ISLANDS, ALTHOUGH IT ORIGINALLY COMES FROM NORTH AFRICA.

SERVES FOUR

INGREDIENTS

   1 whole fish, about 1.2kg/2½lb,
     scaled and cleaned
   10ml/2 tsp coriander seeds
   4 garlic cloves, sliced
   10ml/2 tsp harissa sauce
   90ml/6 tbsp extra virgin
     olive oil
   6 plum tomatoes, sliced
   1 mild onion, sliced
   3 preserved lemons or
     1 fresh lemon
   plenty of fresh herbs, such as bay
     leaves, thyme and rosemary, plus
     extra, to garnish
   salt and ground black pepper

For the sauce
   75ml/3fl oz/⅓ cup light tahini
   juice of 1 lemon
   1 garlic clove, crushed
   45ml/3 tbsp finely chopped
     fresh flat leaf parsley or
     coriander (cilantro)

1 Preheat the oven to 200°C/400°F/ Gas 6. Grease the base and sides of a large shallow ovenproof dish or roasting pan.

2 Slash the fish diagonally three or four times on both sides with a sharp knife. Cut deeply, right in to the backbone.

3 Finely crush the coriander seeds in a pestle and mortar, add the chopped garlic and crush until it has blended into a fine paste. Mix with the harissa sauce and about 60ml/4 tbsp of the extra virgin olive oil.

4 Spread a little of the harissa, coriander and garlic paste inside the cavity of the fish. Spread the remainder over each side of the fish and set aside.

5 Spread the tomatoes, onion and preserved or fresh lemon in the dish. (Thinly slice the lemon if using fresh.) Sprinkle with the remaining oil and season with salt and pepper. Lay the fish on top and tuck plenty of herbs around it. Bake uncovered for 25 minutes, until the fish has turned opaque. Test by piercing the thickest part with a knife.

6 To make the sauce, put all the ingredients in a small pan with 120ml/ 4fl oz/½ cup water and add a little salt and pepper. Cook gently until smooth and heated through. Transfer the fish, lemons and vegetables to a platter, garnish with herbs and serve with the sauce.

COOK'S TIP
If you can't get a suitable large fish, use small whole fish such as red mullet or even cod or haddock steaks. Remember to reduce the cooking time slightly.

Energy 500Kcal/2,083kJ; Protein 43.8g; Carbohydrate 6.9g, of which sugars 6.4g; Fat 33.2g, of which saturates 4.9g; Cholesterol 160mg; Calcium 426mg; Fibre 4g; Sodium 161mg.

POULTRY AND MEAT

Recipes for poultry and meat in Greece always include lots of other flavours: herbs, spices, fruit and nuts, and vegetables. Food is often cooked over an open fire, and skewered meat is widely enjoyed. Stews and casseroles range from a simple Chicken Casserole with Olives, to Meatballs in Rich Tomato Sauce. Traditional roasts include a juicy Roast Chicken with Potatoes and Lemon and robust Roast Lamb with Figs. Serve with vegetables cooked in a rich and mouthwatering sauce created by the olive oil and juices from the meat.

SPICY CHICKEN CASSEROLE WITH RED WINE

THIS IS THE TRADITIONAL CHICKEN DISH ON THE ISLANDS. IT IS USUALLY SERVED WITH PLAIN RICE OR ORZO, THE SMALL TEAR-SHAPED PASTA, WHICH IS CALLED KRITHARAKI IN GREEK, BUT IT IS EVEN BETTER WITH THICK HOME-MADE FRIED POTATOES OR HOMEFRIES.

SERVES FOUR

INGREDIENTS

75ml/5 tbsp extra virgin
   olive oil
1.6kg/3½lb organic or free-range
   chicken, jointed
1 large onion, peeled and
   roughly chopped
250ml/8fl oz/1 cup
   red wine
30ml/2 tbsp tomato purée (paste)
   diluted in 450ml/¾ pint/
   scant 2 cups hot water
1 cinnamon stick
3 or 4 whole allspice
2 bay leaves
salt and ground black pepper
boiled rice, orzo or fried potatoes,
   to serve

1 Heat the olive oil in a large pan or sauté pan and brown the chicken pieces on all sides, ensuring that the skin is cooked and lifts away from the flesh slightly. Lift the chicken pieces out with tongs and set them aside on a plate, cover with another plate or with foil and keep them warm.

2 Add the chopped onion to the hot oil in the same pan and stir it over a medium heat until the onions become translucent.

VARIATION
If you have trouble finding this Greek pasta, you can use Italian pasta. Look for a small pasta shape. Long-grained rice can also be used instead of the pasta, if you prefer.

3 Return the chicken pieces to the pan, pour over the wine and cook for 2–3 minutes, until it has reduced. Add the tomato purée mixture, cinnamon, allspice and bay leaves. Season well with salt and pepper. Cover the pan and cook gently for 1 hour or until the chicken is tender. Serve with rice, orzo or fried potatoes.

Energy 669Kcal/2,775kJ; Protein 48.7g; Carbohydrate 5g, of which sugars 3.8g; Fat 45.9g, of which saturates 11.1g; Cholesterol 250mg; Calcium 37mg; Fibre 0.9g; Sodium 196mg.

CHARGRILLED CHICKEN <u>WITH</u> GARLIC <u>AND</u> PEPPERS

AN IMAGINATIVE MARINADE CAN MAKE ALL THE DIFFERENCE TO THE SOMETIMES BLAND FLAVOUR OF CHICKEN. THIS GARLICKY MARINADE, WITH MUSTARD AND CHILLI, GIVES TENDER CHICKEN A REAL PUNCH. MAKE SURE THE CHICKEN HAS PLENTY OF TIME TO ABSORB THE FLAVOURS BEFORE COOKING.

SERVES FOUR TO SIX

INGREDIENTS
   1½ chickens, total weight
      about 2.25kg/5lb, jointed,
      or 12 chicken pieces
   2 or 3 red or green (bell) peppers,
      quartered and seeded
   4 or 5 ripe tomatoes, halved
      horizontally
   lemon wedges, to serve

For the marinade
   90ml/6 tbsp extra virgin
      olive oil
   juice of 1 large lemon
   5ml/1 tsp French mustard
   4 garlic cloves, crushed
   2 fresh red or green chillies,
      seeded and chopped
   5ml/1 tsp dried oregano
   salt and ground black pepper

COOK'S TIP
You can, of course, cook these under the grill (broiler). Have the heat fairly high, but don't place the pieces of chicken too close to the heat. The chicken will probably need less time than when cooked over the coals – allow about 15 minutes each side.

1 If you are jointing the chicken yourself, divide the legs into two. Make a couple of slits in the deepest part of the flesh of each piece of chicken, using a small sharp knife. This will help the marinade to be absorbed more efficiently and will also let the chicken cook thoroughly.

2 Beat together all the marinade ingredients in a large bowl. Add the chicken pieces and turn them over to coat them thoroughly in the marinade. Cover the bowl with clear film (plastic wrap) and place in the refrigerator for 4–8 hours, turning the chicken pieces over in the marinade a couple of times, if possible.

3 Prepare the barbecue. When the coals are ready, lift the chicken pieces out of the marinade and place them on the grill. Add the pepper pieces and the tomatoes to the marinade and set it aside for 15 minutes. Grill the chicken pieces for 20–25 minutes. Watch them closely and move them away from the area where the heat is most fierce if they start to burn.

4 Turn the chicken pieces over and cook them for 20–25 minutes more. Meanwhile, thread the peppers on two long metal skewers. Add them to the barbecue grill, with the tomatoes, for the last 15 minutes of cooking. Remember to keep an eye on them and turn them over at least once. Serve with the lemon wedges.

Energy 760Kcal/3,156kJ; Protein 61.7g; Carbohydrate 11.1g, of which sugars 10.8g; Fat 52.2g, of which saturates 13.3g; Cholesterol 313mg; Calcium 40mg; Fibre 3.1g; Sodium 235mg.

CHICKEN CASSEROLE WITH OLIVES

THIS IS A VERY SIMPLE DISH TO PREPARE AND COOK, BUT WITH ITS TYPICAL MEDITERRANEAN UNDERTONES IT IS ALSO FULL OF FLAVOUR. IT IS DELICIOUS SERVED WITH FRENCH FRIES OR PLAIN BOILED RICE, BUT IT GOES EQUALLY WELL WITH BOILED NEW POTATOES.

SERVES FOUR

INGREDIENTS
  75ml/5 tbsp extra virgin
    olive oil
  1 organic or free-range
    chicken, about 1.6kg/3½lb,
    jointed
  3 or 4 shallots, finely chopped
  2 carrots, sliced
  1 celery stick, roughly chopped
  2 garlic cloves, chopped
  juice of 1 lemon
  300ml/½ pint/1¼ cups hot water
  30ml/2 tbsp chopped
    flat leaf parsley
  12 black or green olives
  salt and ground black pepper

1 Preheat the oven to 180°C/350°F/ Gas 4. Heat the olive oil in a wide flameproof casserole and brown the chicken pieces on both sides. Lift them out and set them aside.

2 Add the shallots, carrots and celery to the oil remaining in the casserole and sauté them for a few minutes. Stir in the garlic. As soon as it becomes aromatic, return the chicken to the pan and pour the lemon juice over the mixture. Let it bubble for a few minutes, then add the water and season with salt and pepper.

3 Cover the casserole and bake for 1 hour, turning the chicken pieces over occasionally.

4 Remove the casserole from the oven and stir in the parsley and olives. Re-cover the casserole and return it to the oven for about 30 minutes more. Check that it is cooked by piercing with a sharp knife. The juices should run clear. Serve immediately.

Energy 726Kcal/3,008kJ; Protein 54.9g; Carbohydrate 3.8g, of which sugars 3.5g; Fat 54.5g, of which saturates 13.1g; Cholesterol 289mg; Calcium 55mg; Fibre 1.9g; Sodium 435mg.

ROAST CHICKEN WITH POTATOES AND LEMON

THIS IS A LOVELY, EASY DISH FOR A FAMILY MEAL. AS WITH OTHER GREEK ROASTS, EVERYTHING IS BAKED TOGETHER SO THAT THE POTATOES ABSORB ALL THE DIFFERENT FLAVOURS, ESPECIALLY THAT OF THE LEMON AND THE LOVELY JUICES AND FATS FROM THE CHICKEN.

SERVES FOUR

INGREDIENTS

    1 organic or free-range chicken, about 1.6kg/3½lb
    2 garlic cloves, peeled but left whole
    15ml/1 tbsp chopped fresh thyme or oregano, or 5ml/1 tsp dried, plus 2 or 3 fresh sprigs of thyme or oregano
    800g/1¾lb potatoes
    juice of 1 lemon
    60ml/4 tbsp extra virgin olive oil
    300ml/½ pint/1¼ cups hot water
    salt and ground black pepper

1 Preheat the oven to 200°C/400°F/ Gas 6. Place the chicken, breast-side down, in a large roasting pan, then tuck the garlic cloves and the fresh thyme or oregano sprigs inside and around the bird.

2 Peel the potatoes and quarter them lengthways. If they are very large, slice them lengthways into thinner pieces. Arrange the potatoes around the chicken, then pour the lemon juice over the chicken and potatoes.

3 Season the chicken and potatoes with salt and freshly ground black pepper. Drizzle the olive oil over the top and add about three-quarters of the fresh or dried chopped thyme or oregano. Pour the hot water into the roasting pan.

4 Roast the chicken and potatoes for 30 minutes, then remove the roasting pan from the oven and carefully turn the chicken over. Baste, season the bird with a little more salt and pepper, sprinkle over the remaining fresh or dried herbs, and add more hot water, if needed. Reduce the oven temperature to 190°C/375°F/Gas 5.

5 Return the chicken and potatoes to the oven and roast them for another hour, or slightly longer, by which time both the chicken and the potatoes will be a golden colour. Serve with a crisp leafy salad, if you like.

Energy 767Kcal/3,195kJ; Protein 53.3g; Carbohydrate 32.5g, of which sugars 2.9g; Fat 47.7g, of which saturates 11.8g; Cholesterol 264mg; Calcium 51mg; Fibre 2.6g; Sodium 206mg.

SPRING LAMB CASSEROLE WITH FRESH PEAS

IN GREECE, MILK-FED LAMB IS AT ITS BEST IN APRIL AND MAY, WHICH IS ABOUT THE TIME WHEN FRESH PEAS PUT IN AN APPEARANCE IN THE MARKETS. HERE, PEAS AND LAMB ARE COMBINED TO PRODUCE ONE OF THE MOST DELICIOUS GREEK DISHES — A REAL TREAT.

SERVES FOUR TO SIX

INGREDIENTS

75ml/5 tbsp extra virgin olive oil
4–6 thick shoulder of lamb steaks,
    with the bone in
1 large onion, thinly sliced
5 or 6 spring onions (scallions),
    roughly chopped
2 carrots, sliced in rounds
juice of 1 lemon
1.2kg/2½lb fresh peas in pods,
    shelled (this will yield about
    500–675g/1¼–1½lb peas)
60ml/4 tbsp finely chopped fresh dill
salt and ground black pepper

1 Heat the olive oil in a wide, heavy pan. Brown the lamb on both sides. Lift the pieces out, and set them to one side.

2 Sauté the onion slices in the oil remaining in the pan until they are translucent. Add the chopped spring onions and, 1 minute later, the sliced carrots. Sauté for 3–4 minutes, until slightly tender.

COOK'S TIP
In Greek cooking, meat is always cooked well so that it is tender and almost falling away from the bone.

3 Return the lamb steaks to the pan, pour the lemon juice over them and let it evaporate for a few seconds. Pour over enough hot water to cover the meat. Add salt and pepper. Cover and simmer for 45–50 minutes, or until the meat is almost tender, turning the steaks over and stirring the vegetables from time to time.

4 Add the peas and half the dill, with a little more water, if needed. Replace the lid and cook for 20–30 minutes, or until the meat and vegetables are fully cooked. Sprinkle the remaining dill over the casserole just before serving.

Energy 858Kcal/3,551kJ; Protein 40.2g; Carbohydrate 29g, of which sugars 11.8g; Fat 65.6g, of which saturates 26.9g; Cholesterol 119mg; Calcium 79mg; Fibre 10.2g; Sodium 132mg.

MEATBALLS IN RICH TOMATO SAUCE

THIS IS A PRACTICAL ALL-IN-ONE DISH THAT IS VERY EASY TO MAKE. THERE ARE DIFFERENT VERSIONS OF YIOUVARLAKIA, OR MEATBALLS. THIS ONE, WITH ITS RICH TOMATO SAUCE, IS IDEAL IN THE AUTUMN AS IT SEEMS TO BRING BACK ECHOES OF SUMMER WITH ITS SWEETNESS.

SERVES FOUR

INGREDIENTS
- 500g/1¼lb/2½ cups minced (ground) lamb or beef
- 1 onion, grated
- 1 egg, lightly beaten
- 50g/2oz/generous ⅓ cup short grain rice
- 45ml/3 tbsp chopped flat leaf parsley
- finely grated rind of ½ orange, plus extra to garnish (optional)
- extra virgin olive oil, for frying
- salt and freshly ground black pepper
- fresh crusty bread, to serve

For the sauce
- 60ml/4 tbsp extra virgin olive oil
- 1 onion, thinly sliced
- 3–4 fresh sage leaves, finely sliced
- 400g/14oz can tomatoes
- 300ml/½ pint/1¼ cups beef stock or hot water

1 Put the meat in a bowl and add the onion, egg, rice and parsley. Add the grated orange rind to the mixture with salt and pepper. Mix all the ingredients well, then shape the mixture into round balls or small sausage shapes.

2 Heat some olive oil in a large, flat frying pan over a medium heat. When the oil is hot, add the sausages one by one, gently rolling them over to brown the outsides. Take care not to break up the sausages as they can be quite fragile at this stage. Brown around the edges and then remove and set aside.

3 To make the sauce, heat the oil in a wide pan that will take the meatballs in one layer. Sauté the onion slices until they just start to become golden. Add the sage, then the tomatoes, breaking them up with a wooden spoon.

4 Simmer for a few minutes, then add the stock or water, turn up the heat and bring to the boil.

5 Lower the meatballs gently into the sauce. Do not stir but rotate the pan to coat them evenly. Take care not to break them up.

6 Season with salt and freshly ground black pepper, then cover the pan and simmer for about 30 minutes, or until the sauce has thickened. Transfer to a serving platter and sprinkle over a little orange rind to garnish, if you like. Serve with lots of crusty bread to mop up all the juices.

Energy 475Kcal/1,972kJ; Protein 28.5g; Carbohydrate 15.8g, of which sugars 5.1g; Fat 33.2g, of which saturates 10.7g; Cholesterol 123mg; Calcium 58mg; Fibre 2g; Sodium 131mg.

ROAST LAMB <u>WITH</u> FIGS

LAMB FILLET IS AN EXPENSIVE CUT OF MEAT, BUT BECAUSE IT IS VERY LEAN THERE IS VERY LITTLE LEFT TO WASTE. TO MAKE A MORE ECONOMICAL VERSION OF THIS DISH, YOU CAN USE LEG OF LAMB INSTEAD. IT HAS A STRONGER FLAVOUR BUT IS JUST AS DELICIOUS. SERVE WITH FRESHLY STEAMED GREEN BEANS WITH NEW POTATOES FOR A SUBSTANTIAL SUPPER.

SERVES SIX

INGREDIENTS
　　30ml/2 tbsp extra virgin
　　　olive oil
　　1kg/2¼lb lamb fillet, trimmed
　　　of excess fat
　　9 fresh figs
　　150ml/¼ pint/⅔ cup ruby port
　　salt and ground black pepper
　　a few sprigs of fresh parsley,
　　　to garnish
　　new potatoes and green beans,
　　　to serve

1 Preheat the oven to 190°C/375°F/ Gas 5. Heat the olive oil in a large roasting pan over a medium heat until the oil is hot and sizzling.

2 Fry the lamb fillet and sear on all sides until evenly browned.

3 Cut the fresh figs in half and arrange them around the lamb. Season the lamb with salt and ground black pepper and roast in the oven for 30 minutes. Pour the port over the figs.

4 Return the lamb to the oven for a further 30–45 minutes. The meat should be slightly pink in the centre.

5 Transfer the lamb to a board and leave to rest for about 5 minutes. Carve into slices, garnish with parsley and serve with new potatoes and green beans.

Energy 517Kcal/2,170kJ; Protein 35.4g; Carbohydrate 41.1g, of which sugars 41.1g; Fat 23.6g, of which saturates 9.2g; Cholesterol 127mg; Calcium 204mg; Fibre 5.7g; Sodium 191mg.

BAKED LAMB <u>WITH</u> TOMATOES, GARLIC <u>AND</u> PASTA

A LAMB YIOUVETSI IS UNDOUBTEDLY VERY SPECIAL IN GREECE. IT IS ONE OF THE MOST POPULAR DISHES AND IS OFTEN MADE FOR THE AUSPICIOUS CELEBRATORY FAMILY LUNCH ON 15 AUGUST, AN IMPORTANT DATE IN THE GREEK ORTHODOX CALENDAR AS IT MARKS THE FEAST OF THE ASSUMPTION OF THE VIRGIN MARY AND THE END OF THE LONG FASTING PERIOD THROUGH THE SUMMER MONTHS.

SERVES SIX

INGREDIENTS

1 shoulder of lamb, most of the fat removed, sliced into serving portions
600g/1lb 6oz ripe tomatoes, peeled and chopped, or 400g/14oz can chopped plum tomatoes
4 or 5 garlic cloves, chopped
75ml/5 tbsp extra virgin olive oil
5ml/1 tsp dried oregano
1 litre/1¾ pints/4 cups hot water
400g/14oz/3½ cups orzo pasta, or spaghetti, broken into short lengths
salt and ground black pepper
50g/2oz/½ cup freshly grated Kefalotiri or Parmesan cheese, to serve

VARIATION
The dish can also be made with young goat (kid) or beef, but these have to be boiled first.

1 Preheat the oven to 190°C/375°F/ Gas 5. Rinse the meat to remove any obvious bone splinters, and place it in a large roasting pan.

2 Add the fresh or canned tomatoes, and the crushed garlic, extra virgin olive oil and dried oregano. Season with salt and freshly ground black pepper and stir in 300ml/½ pint/1¼ cups of the hot water.

3 Place the lamb in the oven and bake for about 1 hour 10 minutes, basting and turning the meat twice.

4 Remove the lamb from the oven and reduce the oven temperature to 180°C/350°F/Gas 4. Add the remaining 700ml/scant 1¼ pints/2¾ cups hot water to the roasting pan. Stir in the pasta and add more seasoning.

5 Mix well, return the roasting pan to the oven and bake for 30–40 minutes more, stirring occasionally, until the meat is fully cooked and tender, and the pasta feels soft.

6 Serve immediately, with a bowl of grated cheese to be sprinkled over individual portions.

COOK'S TIPS
• As *yiouvetsi* is quite a rich dish, it is a good idea to accompany it with a salad, to refresh the palate.
• If possible, use ripe vine tomatoes, as it is their flavour that really makes the difference.

Energy 528Kcal/2,222kJ; Protein 31.8g; Carbohydrate 52.5g, of which sugars 5.3g; Fat 22.7g, of which saturates 7.8g; Cholesterol 100mg; Calcium 131mg; Fibre 2.9g; Sodium 156mg.

GRILLED SKEWERED LAMB

LAMB STILL MAKES THE BEST SOUVLAKIA – KEBABS – BUT IN GREECE THIS HAS NOW LARGELY BEEN REPLACED BY PORK, WHICH IS CONSIDERABLY CHEAPER. SOUVLAKIA ARE AT THEIR BEST SERVED WITH TZATSIKI, A LARGE TOMATO SALAD AND BARBECUED BREAD.

SERVES FOUR TO SIX

INGREDIENTS

    1 small shoulder of lamb, boned and
      with most of the fat removed
    2 or 3 onions, preferably red onions,
      quartered
    2 red or green (bell) peppers,
      quartered and seeded
    75ml/5 tbsp extra virgin olive oil
    juice of 1 lemon
    2 garlic cloves, crushed
    5ml/1 tsp dried oregano
    2.5ml/½ tsp dried thyme or some
      sprigs of fresh thyme
    salt and ground black pepper

1 Put the olive oil, lemon juice, crushed garlic and herbs in a large bowl. Season with salt and pepper and whisk well to combine. Add the meat cubes, stirring to coat them in the mixture.

2 Cover the bowl tightly and leave to marinate for 4–8 hours in the refrigerator, stirring several times.

3 Separate the onion quarters into pieces, each composed of two or three layers, and slice each pepper quarter in half widthways.

4 Lift out the meat cubes, reserving the marinade, and thread them on to long metal skewers, alternating each piece of meat with a piece of pepper and a piece of onion. Lay them across a grill pan or baking tray and brush them with the reserved marinade.

5 Preheat a grill (broiler) until hot, or prepare a barbecue. Cook the *souvlakia* under a medium to high heat or over the hot coals for 10 minutes, until they start to become scorched. If using the grill, do not place them too close to the heat source. Turn the skewers over, brush again with the marinade (or a little olive oil) and cook for 10–15 minutes more. Serve immediately.

COOK'S TIPS

• Ask your butcher to trim the meat and cut it into 4cm/1½in cubes. A little fat is desirable with *souvlakia*, as it keeps them moist and succulent during cooking. If you prefer, you can use 4–5 best end neck (cross rib) fillets instead of shoulder.

• If you are barbecuing the *souvlakia* you may need to cook them for slightly longer, depending on the intensity of the heat.

Energy 415Kcal/1,724kJ; Protein 31.2g; Carbohydrate 9.6g, of which sugars 8.1g; Fat 28.2g, of which saturates 8.8g; Cholesterol 138mg; Calcium 31mg; Fibre 2.1g; Sodium 86mg.

GREEK LAMB SAUSAGES WITH TOMATO SAUCE

THE GREEK NAME FOR THESE SAUSAGES IS SOUZOUKAKIA. THEY ARE MORE LIKE ELONGATED MEATBALLS THAN THE TYPE OF SAUSAGE WE ARE ACCUSTOMED TO. THEY CAN BE SERVED WITH PASTA, RICE OR FRESH, CRUSTY BREAD, ACCOMPANIED BY A GREEN OR MIXED SALAD.

SERVES FOUR

INGREDIENTS

50g/2oz/1 cup fresh
 breadcrumbs
150ml/¼ pint/⅔ cup milk
675g/1½lb/3 cups minced
 (ground) lamb
30ml/2 tbsp grated onion
3 garlic cloves, crushed
10ml/2 tsp ground cumin
30ml/2 tbsp chopped fresh
 flat leaf parsley
flour, for dusting
olive oil, for frying
600ml/1 pint/2½ cups
 passata (bottled,
 strained tomatoes)
5ml/1 tsp sugar
2 bay leaves
1 small onion, peeled
salt and ground black pepper
a few sprigs of fresh flat leaf
 parsley, to garnish

1 Mix together the breadcrumbs and milk. Add the minced lamb, onion, garlic, cumin and chopped parsley and season well with salt and freshly ground black pepper.

2 Shape the mixture with your hands into little fat sausages, about 5cm/2in long, and roll them in flour. Heat about 60ml/4 tbsp olive oil in a frying pan.

VARIATION
The sausages can also be made with minced (ground) beef.

3 Fry the sausages for about 8 minutes, turning them frequently until they are evenly browned all over. Remove from the pan and drain on a plate covered with a few sheets of kitchen paper.

4 Put the passata, sugar, bay leaves and whole onion in a pan and simmer for 20 minutes. Add the sausages and cook for 10 minutes more. Serve garnished with parsley.

Energy 477Kcal/1,990kJ; Protein 35.3g; Carbohydrate 13.8g, of which sugars 3.8g; Fat 31.6g, of which saturates 12.1g; Cholesterol 132mg; Calcium 98mg; Fibre 0.7g; Sodium 229mg.

BEEF CASSEROLE WITH BABY ONIONS

This is the perfect Sunday lunch for a family, but is also an excellent choice for a dinner party. Moshari stifado is an unusual but mouthwatering dish, with the small pickling-size onions melting in the mouth with sweetness.

SERVES FOUR

INGREDIENTS

75ml/5 tbsp olive oil
1kg/2¼lb good stewing or braising
  steak, cut into large cubes
3 garlic cloves, chopped
5ml/1 tsp ground cumin
5cm/2in piece of cinnamon stick
175ml/6fl oz/¾ cup red wine
30ml/2 tbsp red wine vinegar
small sprig of fresh rosemary
2 bay leaves, crumbled
30ml/2 tbsp tomato purée (paste)
  diluted in 1 litre/1¾ pints/4 cups
  hot water
675g/1½lb small pickling-size
  onions, peeled and left whole
15ml/1 tbsp demerara (raw) sugar
salt and freshly ground
  black pepper

1 Heat the olive oil in a large, heavy pan and brown the meat cubes, in batches if necessary, until pale golden brown all over.

2 Stir in the garlic and cumin. Add the cinnamon stick and cook for a few seconds, then pour the wine and vinegar slowly over the mixture. Let the liquid bubble and evaporate for 3–4 minutes.

3 Add the rosemary and bay leaves, with the diluted tomato purée. Stir well, season with salt and pepper, then cover and simmer gently for about 1½ hours or until the meat is tender.

4 Dot the onions over the meat mixture and shake the pan to distribute them evenly. Sprinkle the demerara sugar over the onions, cover the pan and cook very gently for 30 minutes, until the onions are soft but have not begun to disintegrate. If necessary, add a little hot water at this stage. Do not stir once the onions have been added but gently shake the pan instead to coat them in the sauce. Remove the cinnamon stick and sprig of rosemary and serve.

COOK'S TIP
Stifado can be cooked in the oven, if you prefer. Use a flameproof casserole. Having browned the meat and added the remaining ingredients, with the exception of the onions and sugar, transfer the covered casserole to an oven preheated to 160°C/325°F/Gas 3 and bake for about 2 hours, or until the meat is tender. Add the onions and sugar as above and return the casserole to the oven for 1 hour more.

Energy 672Kcal/2,798kJ; Protein 59.2g; Carbohydrate 18.4g, of which sugars 14.5g; Fat 37.4g, of which saturates 11.5g; Cholesterol 145mg; Calcium 62mg; Fibre 2.6g; Sodium 186mg.

BEEF AND AUBERGINE CASSEROLE

EASY TO MAKE BUT WITH AN EXOTIC TASTE, THIS WOULD MAKE AN EXCELLENT MAIN COURSE FOR A DINNER PARTY. USE GOOD-QUALITY BEEF AND COOK IT SLOWLY, SO THAT IT IS MELTINGLY TENDER AND FULL OF FLAVOUR. SERVE WITH TOASTED PITTA BREAD.

SERVES FOUR

INGREDIENTS

60ml/4 tbsp extra virgin olive oil
1kg/2¼lb good-quality stewing
 steak or feather steak, sliced in
 4 thick pieces
1 onion, chopped
2.5ml/½ tsp dried oregano
2 garlic cloves, chopped
175ml/6fl oz/¾ cup white wine
400g/14oz can chopped
 tomatoes
2 or 3 aubergines (eggplants), total
 weight about 675g/1½lb
150ml/¼ pint/⅔ cup
 sunflower oil
45ml/3 tbsp finely chopped
 fresh parsley
salt and freshly ground
 black pepper
toasted pitta bread and green or
 mixed salad, to serve

1 Heat the olive oil in a large pan and brown the pieces of meat on both sides. As each piece browns, take it out and set it aside on a plate.

2 Add the onion to the oil remaining in the pan and sauté until translucent. Add the oregano and the garlic, then, as soon as the garlic becomes aromatic, return the meat to the pan and pour the wine over. Allow the wine to bubble and evaporate for a few minutes, then add the tomatoes, with enough hot water to just cover the meat. Bring to the boil, lower the heat, cover and cook for about 1 hour, until the meat is tender.

3 Meanwhile, trim the aubergines and slice them into 2cm/¾in thick rounds, then slice each round in half. Heat the sunflower oil and fry the aubergines briefly in batches over a high heat, turning them over as they become light golden. They do not have to cook at this stage and should not be allowed to burn. Lift them out and drain them on kitchen paper. When all the aubergines have been fried, season them.

4 When the meat feels tender, season it with salt and freshly ground black pepper. Then add the aubergine pieces and shake the pan to distribute them evenly. From this point, do not stir the mixture as the aubergines will be quite fragile and you need to avoid breaking the pieces up.

5 Add a little more hot water so that the aubergines are submerged in the sauce, cover the pan and simmer for 30 minutes more, or until the meat is very tender and all the flavours have amalgamated.

6 Sprinkle the parsley over the top and simmer gently for a few more minutes before transferring to a serving platter or dish. Serve with hot toasted pitta bread tucked into the folds of a warm, clean dish towel, and accompany with a fresh green or mixed salad.

Energy 838Kcal/3,479kJ; Protein 59.2g; Carbohydrate 8.3g, of which sugars 7.6g; Fat 60.2g, of which saturates 14.4g; Cholesterol 145mg; Calcium 44mg; Fibre 4.6g; Sodium 175mg.

PORK WITH CHICKPEAS AND ORANGE

THIS WINTER SPECIALITY IS A FAMILIAR DISH IN THE AEGEAN ISLANDS, PARTICULARLY IN CRETE.
IN THE VILLAGES OF MESARA IT IS TRADITIONALLY OFFERED TO FAMILY AND CLOSE FRIENDS ON THE
NIGHT BEFORE A WEDDING. THIS VERSION COMES FROM THE ISLAND OF CHIOS. ALL YOU NEED TO
SERVE WITH THIS LOVELY DISH IS FRESH BREAD AND A BOWL OF BLACK OLIVES.

SERVES FOUR

INGREDIENTS
   350g/12oz/1¾ cups dried chickpeas,
     soaked overnight in water to cover
   75–90ml/5–6 tbsp extra virgin
     olive oil
   675g/1½lb boneless leg of pork,
     cut into large cubes
   1 large onion, sliced
   2 garlic cloves, chopped
   400g/14oz can chopped tomatoes
   grated rind of 1 orange
   1 small dried red chilli
   salt and ground black pepper

1 Drain the chickpeas, rinse them under cold water and drain them again. Place them in a large, heavy pan. Pour in enough cold water to cover generously, put a lid on the pan and bring to the boil.

2 Skim the surface, replace the lid and cook gently for 1–1½ hours, depending on the age and pedigree of the chickpeas. Alternatively, cook them in a pressure cooker for 20 minutes under full pressure. When the chickpeas are soft, drain them, reserving the cooking liquid, and set them aside.

3 Heat the olive oil in the clean pan and brown the meat cubes in batches. As each cube browns, lift it out with a slotted spoon and put it on a plate. When all the meat cubes have been browned, add the onion to the oil remaining in the pan and sauté the slices until light golden. Stir in the garlic, then as soon as it becomes aromatic, add the tomatoes and orange rind.

4 Crumble in the chilli. Return the chickpeas and meat to the pan, and pour in enough of the reserved cooking liquid to cover. Add the black pepper, but not salt at this stage.

5 Mix well, cover the pan and simmer for about 1 hour, or until the meat is tender. Stir occasionally and add more of the reserved liquid if needed. The result should be a moist casserole; not soupy, but not dry either. Season with salt before serving.

Energy 663Kcal/2,781kJ; Protein 56.7g; Carbohydrate 54.4g, of which sugars 11g; Fat 25.7g, of which saturates 4.9g; Cholesterol 106mg; Calcium 184mg; Fibre 11.8g; Sodium 164mg.

SPICY SAUSAGE AND PEPPER STEW

THIS DISH, SPETZOFAI, IS A SPECIALITY OF THE PELION ON THE EASTERN COAST OF GREECE. THE BEAUTIFUL MOUNTAIN RANGE TOWERS OVER THE CITY OF VOLOS ON ONE SIDE AND THE FRESH BLUE AEGEAN ON THE OTHER. YOU WILL FIND SPETZOFAI IN ALL ITS PICTURE-POSTCARD VILLAGES, BUT IT IS ALSO POPULAR ON ALL THE NEARBY ISLANDS OF SKIATHOS, ALONNISOS AND SKOPELOS.

SERVES FOUR

INGREDIENTS

675g/1½lb red and green (bell) peppers
75ml/5 tbsp extra virgin olive oil
500g/1¼lb spicy sausages (Italian garlic sausages, Merguez or Toulouse if you cannot find Greek sausages)
400g/14oz tomatoes, skinned and roughly sliced
5ml/1 tsp dried oregano or some fresh thyme, chopped
150ml/¼ pint/⅔ cup hot water
45ml/3 tbsp chopped fresh flat leaf parsley
salt and ground black pepper
chopped fresh thyme, to garnish

1 Halve and seed the peppers and cut them into quarters. Heat the olive oil in a large, heavy pan, add the peppers and sauté them over a medium heat for 10–15 minutes until they start to brown.

2 Meanwhile, slice the sausages into bitesize chunks. Then carefully tip the hot olive oil into a frying pan.

3 Add the sausages and fry them briefly, turning them frequently, to get rid of the excess fat but not to cook them. As soon as they are brown, remove from the pan with a slotted spoon and drain on kitchen paper.

4 Add the tomatoes, sausages and herbs to the peppers. Stir in the water and season with salt and pepper, then cover the pan and cook gently for about 30 minutes. Mix in the chopped parsley and serve piping hot.

COOK'S TIP
If you prefer, stir in the parsley, spread the mixture in a medium baking dish and bake in an oven preheated to 180°C/350°F/Gas 4. Cook for about 40 minutes, stirring occasionally.

Energy 573Kcal/2,378kJ; Protein 14.8g; Carbohydrate 28.9g, of which sugars 15.9g; Fat 45g, of which saturates 14.7g; Cholesterol 50mg; Calcium 106mg; Fibre 5g; Sodium 1,033mg.

VEGETARIAN MEALS

Pulses, vegetables, eggs and cheese feature strongly in Greek cuisine,

reflecting the abundance of fresh produce that is grown and produced

both on the mainland and on the islands. Herbs gathered wild from the

countryside are used plentifully, imparting their own distinctive

flavours. There are some tempting vegetarian dishes to be had — try a

simple Cheese and Leek Pie, an aromatic Courgette and Potato Bake,

or delicious Halloumi with Potatoes.

CHEESE AND LEEK PIE

THIS PIE, WHICH COMES FROM THE SPORADES ISLANDS, IS UNUSUAL BY GREEK STANDARDS BECAUSE IT IS NOT ENCLOSED IN PASTRY. IT IS CALLED TYROPITTA AND IS PERFECT SERVED WITH THE MEZEDES, OR AS A LOVELY LUNCH WITH A FRESH LEAFY GREEN SALAD.

SERVES FOUR

INGREDIENTS
  1 onion, sliced
  50g/2oz/¼ cup butter
  60ml/4 tbsp extra virgin olive oil
  2 large leeks, total weight about
    450g/1lb, chopped
  115g/4oz/1 cup plain
    (all-purpose) flour
  2.5ml/½ tsp bicarbonate of soda
    (baking soda)
  3 large (US extra large) eggs,
    lightly beaten
  200g/7oz/scant 1 cup Greek
    (US strained plain) yogurt
  300g/11oz feta cheese, cubed
  115g/4oz freshly grated Gruyère or
    Parmesan cheese
  45–60ml/3–4 tbsp chopped fresh dill
  salt and ground black pepper
  lemon wedges, black olives and
    radishes, to garnish

1 Sauté the onion in the butter and oil until light golden. Add the leeks and cook over a low heat for 10–12 minutes until soft. Cool a little.

2 Preheat the oven to 180°C/350°F/ Gas 4. Lightly grease a 23cm/9in round springform cake tin (pan). Sift the flour and bicarbonate of soda into a bowl. Stir in the eggs, then the yogurt and feta cheese, and finally the leek and onion mixture. Set aside 30ml/2 tbsp of the grated Gruyère or Parmesan cheese and add the rest to the batter, with the dill. Mix well and season.

COOK'S TIP
To remove all the grit from trimmed leeks, cut down through about 10cm/4in of the green part and then turn the leek and cut again, making a cross. Rinse thoroughly in running water.

3 Spoon the mixture into the prepared tin and level the surface. Sprinkle the reserved grated cheese evenly over the top and bake for 40–45 minutes, or until golden brown.

4 Let the pie cool completely before removing it from the tin. Serve in wedges and offer some tasty extra virgin olive oil to be drizzled over the top. Garnish with lemon wedges, black olives and radishes.

Energy 751Kcal/3,124kJ; Protein 35.8g; Carbohydrate 28.9g, of which sugars 5.9g; Fat 56.1g, of which saturates 28.2g; Cholesterol 251mg; Calcium 804mg; Fibre 3.9g; Sodium 1,564mg.

HALLOUMI <u>WITH</u> POTATOES

THIS SALAD CAN BE GRILLED SUCCESSFULLY ON THE STOVETOP, BUT IF YOU ARE PLANNING TO USE THE BARBECUE FOR ANOTHER DISH, USE IT FOR THIS RECIPE, TOO, AND TAKE ADVANTAGE OF THE INITIAL HOT BLAST OF HEAT TO SLIGHTLY CHAR AND SEAL THE CHEESE.

<u>SERVES FOUR</u>

INGREDIENTS
   20 baby new potatoes, total weight about 300g/11oz
   200g/7oz extra-fine green beans, trimmed
   675g/1½lb broad (fava) beans, shelled (about 225g/8oz shelled weight)
   200g/7oz halloumi cheese, cut into 5mm/¼in slices
   1 garlic clove, crushed to a paste with a large pinch of salt
   90ml/6 tbsp olive oil
   5ml/1 tsp cider vinegar or white wine vinegar
   15g/½oz/½ cup fresh basil leaves, shredded
   45ml/3 tbsp chopped fresh savory
   2 spring onions (scallions), finely sliced
   salt and ground black pepper
   4 metal or wooden skewers
   a few sprigs of fresh savory, to garnish

1 Divide the potatoes among the 4 skewers, and thread them on. Heat salted water in a pan large enough to take the skewers and, once boiling, add them. Boil for about 7 minutes, or until almost tender.

2 Add the prepared green beans and cook for 3 minutes more. Tip in the broad (fava) beans and cook for just 2 further minutes.

3 Drain all the vegetables in a large colander. Remove the potatoes, still on their skewers, and set to one side.

4 Refresh the cooked broad beans under plenty of cold running water. Pop each broad bean out of its skin to reveal the bright green inner bean. If they do not pop out easily, they may not have been cooked for long enough. Discard the outer shells. Place the beans in a bowl, cover and set aside.

5 Place the halloumi and the potatoes in a wide dish. Whisk the garlic and oil together with a generous grinding of black pepper. Add to the dish and toss with the halloumi and potato skewers.

6 Place the cheese and the potato skewers in a griddle over medium heat and cook for 2 minutes on each side.

7 Add the cider vinegar to the oil and garlic remaining in the dish and whisk to mix. Toss in the beans, herbs and spring onions, with the cooked halloumi. Serve, with the potato skewers laid alongside.

COOK'S TIPS
• To griddle on the barbecue, rake the coals over to one side once the flames have died down. Position a grill rack over the coals to heat. When the coals are hot, or with a light coating of ash, heat the griddle until a few drops of water sprinkled on to the surface evaporate instantly.
• This dish can be cooked directly on the barbecue. When the coals are medium-hot, sear the vegetables and cheese for 2 minutes on each side.

Energy 404Kcal/1,679kJ; Protein 17.5g; Carbohydrate 22.2g, of which sugars 3.5g; Fat 27.8g, of which saturates 9.4g; Cholesterol 29mg; Calcium 280mg; Fibre 7.3g; Sodium 218mg.

BRAISED BEANS AND LENTILS

THIS LOVELY CRETAN DISH IS WONDERFULLY EASY TO MAKE, BUT IT IS VITAL THAT YOU START
SOAKING THE PULSES AND WHEAT THE DAY BEFORE YOU WANT TO SERVE IT.

SERVES FOUR

INGREDIENTS

200g/7oz/generous 1 cup mixed
  beans and lentils
25g/1oz/2 tbsp whole wheat grains
150ml/¼ pint/⅔ cup extra virgin
  olive oil
1 large onion, finely chopped
2 garlic cloves, crushed
5 or 6 fresh sage leaves, chopped
juice of 1 lemon
3 spring onions (scallions),
  thinly sliced
60–75ml/4–5 tbsp chopped fresh dill
salt and freshly ground black pepper

1 Put the pulses and wheat in a large
bowl and cover with cold water. Leave to
soak overnight.

2 Next day, drain the pulse mixture,
rinse it thoroughly under cold water and
drain again. Put the mixture in a large
pan. Cover with plenty of cold water,
bring to the boil, and cook for about 1½
hours, by which time all the ingredients
will be quite soft and tender. Strain,
reserving 475ml/16fl oz/2 cups of the
cooking liquid. Return the bean mixture
to the clean pan.

3 Heat the oil in a frying pan and fry the
onion until light golden. Add the garlic
and sage. As soon as the garlic becomes
aromatic, add the mixture to the beans.
Stir in the reserved liquid, add plenty
of seasoning and simmer for about
15 minutes, or until the pulses are piping
hot. Stir in the lemon juice, then spoon
into serving bowls, top with a sprinkling
of spring onions and dill, and serve.

Energy 428Kcal/1,788kJ; Protein 13.4g; Carbohydrate 37.7g, of which sugars 4.3g; Fat 26g, of which saturates 3.7g; Cholesterol 0mg; Calcium 62mg; Fibre 3.7g; Sodium 24mg.

SCRAMBLED EGGS WITH TOMATOES

KNOWN IN GREECE AS STRAPATSATHA, THIS DISH MAKES A DELICIOUS LIGHT LUNCH ON A SUNNY DAY. ALL YOU NEED ADD IS A SALAD AND SLICES OF CRISP TOAST OR FRESH BREAD.

SERVES FOUR

INGREDIENTS
    60ml/4 tbsp extra virgin olive oil
    2 or 3 shallots, finely chopped
    675g/1½lb sweet tomatoes,
      roughly chopped
    pinch of dried oregano or 5ml/1 tsp
      chopped fresh thyme
    2.5ml/½ tsp sugar
    6 eggs, lightly beaten
    salt and ground black pepper
    fresh thyme, to garnish

1 Heat the olive oil in a large frying pan and sauté the shallots, stirring occasionally, until they are glistening and translucent.

2 Stir in the chopped tomatoes, dried or fresh herbs and sugar, with salt and freshly ground black pepper to taste. Cook over a low heat for about 15 minutes, stirring occasionally, until most of the liquid has evaporated and the sauce is thick.

3 Add the beaten eggs to the pan and cook for 2–3 minutes, stirring continuously with a wooden spatula in the same way as when making scrambled eggs. The eggs should be just set, but not overcooked. Serve immediately, garnished with fresh thyme.

Energy 245Kcal/1,020kJ; Protein 10.8g; Carbohydrate 7g, of which sugars 6.6g; Fat 19.9g, of which saturates 4.1g; Cholesterol 285mg; Calcium 59mg; Fibre 1.9g; Sodium 121mg.

STUFFED TOMATOES AND PEPPERS

COLOURFUL PEPPERS AND TOMATOES MAKE PERFECT CONTAINERS FOR VARIOUS MEAT AND VEGETABLE STUFFINGS. THIS RICE AND HERB VERSION USES TYPICALLY GREEK INGREDIENTS.

SERVES FOUR

INGREDIENTS
2 large ripe tomatoes
1 green (bell) pepper
1 yellow or orange (bell)
   pepper
60ml/4 tbsp extra virgin olive
   oil, plus extra for sprinkling
2 onions, chopped
2 garlic cloves, crushed
50g/2oz/½ cup blanched
   almonds, chopped
75g/3oz/scant ½ cup long
   grain rice, boiled and
   drained
15g/½oz/½ cup fresh mint,
   roughly chopped
15g/½oz/½ cup fresh flat leaf
   parsley, roughly chopped
25g/1oz/2 tbsp sultanas
   (golden raisins)
45ml/3 tbsp ground almonds
salt and ground black pepper
chopped fresh mixed herbs,
   to garnish

1 Cut the tomatoes in half and scoop out the pulp and seeds using a teaspoon. Drain on kitchen paper with cut sides down. Roughly chop the pulp and seeds.

VARIATION
Small aubergines (eggplants) or large courgettes (zucchini) also make good vegetables for stuffing. Halve and scoop out the centres of the vegetables, then oil the vegetable cases and bake for about 15 minutes. Chop the centres, fry for 2–3 minutes and add to the stuffing mixture. Fill the cases with the stuffing and bake as here.

2 Preheat the oven to 190°C/375°F/ Gas 5. Halve the peppers, leaving the stalks intact. Scoop out the seeds. Brush the peppers with 15ml/1 tbsp of the oil and bake on a baking tray for 15 minutes. Place the peppers and tomatoes in a shallow ovenproof dish and season with salt and freshly ground black pepper.

3 Fry the onions in the remaining oil for 5 minutes, until they are transparent. Add the garlic and chopped almonds and fry for a further minute or two, until you can smell the garlic aroma.

4 Remove the pan from the heat and stir in the rice, chopped tomatoes, mint, parsley and sultanas. Season well with salt and pepper and spoon the mixture into the tomatoes and peppers.

5 Pour 150ml/¼ pint/⅔ cup boiling water around the tomatoes and peppers and bake, uncovered, for 20 minutes. Sprinkle with the ground almonds and sprinkle with a little extra olive oil. Return to the oven and bake for a further 20 minutes, or until turning golden. Serve garnished with fresh herbs.

Energy 437Kcal/1,816kJ; Protein 9.6g; Carbohydrate 37.3g, of which sugars 20g; Fat 28.2g, of which saturates 3.2g; Cholesterol 0mg; Calcium 122mg; Fibre 6.4g; Sodium 22mg.

PEPPERS WITH HALLOUMI AND PINE NUTS

HALLOUMI CHEESE IS CREAMY-TASTING AND HAS A FIRM TEXTURE AND SALTY FLAVOUR THAT CONTRASTS WELL WITH THE SUCCULENT SWEET RED, ORANGE AND YELLOW PEPPERS.

SERVES FOUR

INGREDIENTS
  4 red (bell) peppers
  2 orange or yellow
   (bell) peppers
  60ml/4 tbsp garlic or herb extra
   virgin olive oil
  250g/9oz halloumi cheese
  50g/2oz/½ cup pine nuts

1 Preheat the oven to 220°C/425°F/ Gas 7. Halve the 4 red peppers, including their stalks and leaving the stalks attached. Carefully remove the seeds and other unwanted insides with a sharp knife. Halve and seed the 2 orange or yellow peppers. Chop the flesh finely and set to one side.

2 Place the red pepper halves on a baking sheet and fill with the chopped peppers. Drizzle with half the garlic or herb olive oil and bake for 25 minutes, or until the edges of the peppers are beginning to char.

3 With a sharp knife, dice the cheese into pieces about 1cm/½in cubed.

4 Tuck the cheese in the pepper halves among and on top of the chopped peppers. Sprinkle with the pine nuts and drizzle with the remaining garlic or herb extra virgin olive oil. Bake for a further 15 minutes, or until well browned. Serve warm, with a fresh green or mixed salad and toasted pitta or warm crusty bread.

Energy 506Kcal/2,099kJ; Protein 18.4g; Carbohydrate 32.5g, of which sugars 31g; Fat 34.3g, of which saturates 11.3g; Cholesterol 36mg; Calcium 268mg; Fibre 8.3g; Sodium 267mg.

POTATOES WITH FETA CHEESE AND OLIVES

THINLY SLICED POTATOES ARE COOKED WITH GREEK FETA CHEESE AND BLACK AND GREEN OLIVES IN OLIVE OIL FOR THIS FLAVOURSOME DISH. TOASTED PITTA BREAD AND A GREEN SALAD DRESSED WITH A FRUITY EXTRA VIRGIN OLIVE OIL MAKE IDEAL ACCOMPANIMENTS.

SERVES FOUR

INGREDIENTS
  900g/2lb main-crop potatoes
  150ml/¼ pint/⅔ cup extra virgin
    olive oil
  1 sprig of fresh rosemary
  275g/10oz feta cheese, sliced
    and then crumbled
  115g/4oz/1 cup pitted black and
    green olives
  300ml/½ pint/1¼ cups hot
    vegetable stock
  salt and ground black pepper

COOK'S TIP
A good-quality Greek feta cheese will make all the difference to the warming flavours of this dish.

1 Preheat the oven to 200°C/400°F/ Gas 6. Cook the potatoes in plenty of boiling water for 15 minutes. Drain and cool slightly. Peel the potatoes and cut into thin slices.

2 Brush the base and sides of a shallow 1.5 litre/2½ pint/6¼ cup rectangular ovenproof dish with some of the olive oil.

3 Layer the potatoes in the dish with the rosemary, cheese and olives. Drizzle with the remaining olive oil and pour over the stock. Season with salt and plenty of ground black pepper.

4 Cook for 35 minutes, covering with foil to prevent the potatoes from getting too brown. Serve hot, straight from the dish.

Energy 584Kcal/2,429kJ; Protein 14.8g; Carbohydrate 37.3g, of which sugars 4g; Fat 42.7g, of which saturates 13.7g; Cholesterol 48mg; Calcium 279mg; Fibre 3.1g; Sodium 1662mg.

COURGETTE AND POTATO BAKE

COOK THIS DELICIOUS DISH, KNOWN AS BRIAMI IN GREECE, IN EARLY AUTUMN, AND THE AROMAS SPILLING FROM THE KITCHEN WILL RECALL THE RICH SUMMER TASTES AND COLOURS JUST PAST. IN GREECE, THIS WOULD CONSTITUTE A HEARTY MAIN MEAL, WITH A SALAD, SOME OLIVES AND CHEESE.

SERVES FOUR AS A MAIN COURSE
SIX AS A FIRST COURSE

INGREDIENTS
  675g/1½lb courgettes (zucchini)
  450g/1lb potatoes, peeled and cut
    into chunks
  1 onion, finely sliced
  3 garlic cloves, chopped
  1 large red (bell) pepper, seeded
    and cubed
  400g/14oz can chopped tomatoes
  150ml/¼ pint/⅔ cup extra virgin
    olive oil
  150ml/¼ pint/⅔ cup hot water
  5ml/1 tsp dried oregano
  45ml/3 tbsp chopped fresh flat
    leaf parsley, plus a few extra
    sprigs, to garnish
  salt and ground black pepper

1 Preheat the oven to 190°C/375°F/ Gas 5. Scrape the courgettes lightly under running water to dislodge any grit and then slice them into thin rounds. Put them in a large baking dish and add the chopped potatoes, onion, garlic, red pepper and tomatoes. Mix well, then stir in the olive oil, hot water and dried oregano.

2 Spread the mixture evenly, then season with salt and pepper. Bake for 30 minutes, then stir in the parsley and a little more water.

3 Return to the oven and cook for 1 hour, increasing the temperature to 200°C/400°F/Gas 6 for the final 10–15 minutes, so that the potatoes brown.

Energy 374Kcal/1,554kJ; Protein 6.6g; Carbohydrate 28.6g, of which sugars 11.2g; Fat 26.7g, of which saturates 4g; Cholesterol 0mg; Calcium 86mg; Fibre 5.1g; Sodium 29mg.

SIDE DISHES AND SALADS

The wealth of vegetables available in Greece provides a range of tasty side dishes and salads to accompany main courses. Many can be added to the meze table or eaten as a light lunch or main course. Vegetables are always used as fresh as possible, either straight from the garden or the market.

FRESH GREEN BEANS WITH TOMATO SAUCE

*THIS IS A STANDARD SUMMER DISH IN GREECE AND IS MADE WITH DIFFERENT KINDS OF FRESH BEANS
ACCORDING TO WHAT IS AVAILABLE. IT IS USUALLY ACCOMPANIED BY FETA CHEESE AND FRESH BREAD.*

SERVES FOUR

INGREDIENTS

800g/1¾lb green beans, trimmed
150ml/¼ pint/⅔ cup extra virgin
  olive oil
1 large onion, thinly sliced
2 garlic cloves, chopped
2 small potatoes, peeled and
  chopped into cubes
675g/1½lb tomatoes or a 400g/14oz
  can plum tomatoes, chopped
150ml/¼ pint/⅔ cup hot water
45–60ml/3–4 tbsp chopped
  fresh parsley
salt and ground black pepper

1 If the green beans are very long, cut them in half. Drop them into a bowl of cold water so that they are completely submerged. Leave them to absorb the water for a few minutes.

2 Heat the olive oil in a large pan, add the onion and sauté until translucent. Add the garlic, then, when it becomes aromatic, stir in the potatoes and sauté the mixture for a few minutes.

3 Add the tomatoes and the hot water and cook for 5 minutes. Drain the beans, rinse them and drain again, then add them to the pan with a little salt and pepper to season. Cover and simmer for 30 minutes. Stir in the chopped parsley, with a little more hot water if the mixture looks dry. Cook for 10 minutes more, until the beans are very tender. Serve hot with slices of feta cheese, if you like.

Energy 350Kcal/1,448kJ; Protein 6.6g; Carbohydrate 21.9g, of which sugars 13.4g; Fat 26.9g, of which saturates 4g; Cholesterol 0mg; Calcium 121mg; Fibre 7.7g; Sodium 25mg.

BRAISED ARTICHOKES WITH FRESH PEAS

THIS ARTICHOKE DISH IS UNIQUELY DELICATE. SHELLING FRESH PEAS IS RATHER TIME-CONSUMING BUT THEIR MATCHLESS FLAVOUR MAKES THE TASK VERY WORTHWHILE.

SERVES FOUR

INGREDIENTS

    4 medium to large globe
      artichokes
    juice of 1½ lemons
    150ml/¼ pint/⅔ cup extra virgin
      olive oil
    1 onion, thinly sliced
    4 or 5 spring onions (scallions),
      roughly chopped
    2 carrots, peeled and sliced
      in rounds
    1.2kg/2½lb fresh peas in pods,
      shelled (this will give you about
      500–675g/1¼–1½lb peas)
    450ml/¾ pint/scant 2 cups
      hot water
    60ml/4 tbsp finely chopped
      fresh dill
    salt and ground black pepper
    a few sprigs of fresh dill, to
      garnish

1 Remove and discard the outer leaves of the artichokes. Cut off the top, and cut the artichoke in half lengthways. Scoop out the hairy choke and cut the stalk to 4cm/1½in. Drop the halves into a bowl of water acidulated with about one-third of the lemon juice.

2 Heat the oil in a pan and add the onion and spring onions, and then a minute later, add the carrots. Sauté the mixture for a few seconds, then add the peas and stir for 1–2 minutes.

3 Pour in the remaining lemon juice. Let it bubble and evaporate for a few seconds, then add the hot water and bring to the boil. Drain the artichokes and add them to the pan, with salt and pepper to taste. Cover and cook gently for about 40–45 minutes, stirring occasionally. Add the dill and cook for 5 minutes more, or until the vegetables are beautifully tender. Serve hot or at room temperature.

Energy 384Kcal/1,584kJ; Protein 10.5g; Carbohydrate 25.2g, of which sugars 12.4g; Fat 27.5g, of which saturates 4g; Cholesterol 0mg; Calcium 121mg; Fibre 10g; Sodium 85mg.

GREEK TOMATO AND POTATO BAKE

AN ADAPTATION OF A CLASSIC GREEK DISH, WHICH IS USUALLY COOKED ON THE HOB. THIS RECIPE HAS A RICHER FLAVOUR AS IT IS STOVE-COOKED FIRST AND THEN BAKED IN THE OVEN.

SERVES FOUR

INGREDIENTS
  120ml/4fl oz/½ cup extra virgin
    olive oil
  1 large onion, finely chopped
  3 garlic cloves, crushed
  4 large ripe tomatoes, peeled,
    seeded and chopped
  1kg/2¼lb even-size main-crop
    waxy potatoes
  salt and freshly ground
    black pepper
  a few sprigs of fresh flat leaf
    parsley, to garnish

COOK'S TIP
Make sure that the potatoes are evenly sized and completely coated in the olive oil otherwise they will not cook evenly.

1 Preheat the oven to 180°C/350°F/ Gas 4.

2 Heat the oil in a flameproof casserole. Fry the chopped onion and garlic for 5 minutes, or until softened and just starting to brown.

3 Add the tomatoes to the pan, season and cook for 1 minute.

4 Cut the potatoes into wedges. Add to the pan, stirring well. Cook for 10 minutes. Season again with salt and freshly ground black pepper, and cover with a tight-fitting lid.

5 Place the covered casserole on the middle shelf of the oven and cook for 45 minutes–1 hour. Garnish with a few sprigs of fresh flat leaf parsley.

Energy 399Kcal/1,670kJ; Protein 5.9g; Carbohydrate 49.3g, of which sugars 10.6g; Fat 21.2g, of which saturates 3.2g; Cholesterol 0mg; Calcium 41mg; Fibre 4.6g; Sodium 39mg.

CAULIFLOWER <u>WITH</u> EGG AND LEMON

IN GREECE CAULIFLOWER IS VERY POPULAR AND IS USED IN MANY DIFFERENT WAYS. HERE IT IS TEAMED WITH A LEMON SAUCE, A PERFECT ACCOMPANIMENT FOR KEFTEDES (FRIED MEATBALLS).

<u>SERVES SIX</u>

INGREDIENTS
- 75–90ml/5–6 tbsp extra virgin olive oil
- 1 medium cauliflower, divided into large florets
- 2 eggs
- juice of 1 lemon
- 5ml/1 tsp cornflour (cornstarch), mixed to a cream with a little cold water
- 30ml/2 tbsp chopped fresh flat leaf parsley
- salt

1 Heat the olive oil in a large, heavy pan, add the cauliflower florets and sauté over a medium heat until they start to brown.

2 Pour in enough hot water to almost cover the cauliflower florets, add salt to taste, bring to the boil, then cover the pan and cook for 7–8 minutes until the florets are just soft.

3 Remove the pan from the heat and leave to stand, retaining the hot water and covering the pan tightly to keep in the heat. Meanwhile, make the sauce.

4 Beat the eggs in a bowl, add the lemon juice and cornflour and beat until well mixed. While beating, add a few tablespoons of the hot liquid from the cauliflower. Pour the egg mixture slowly over the cauliflower, then stir gently. Place the pan over a very gentle heat for 2 minutes to thicken the sauce. Spoon into a warmed serving bowl, sprinkle the chopped parsley over the top and serve.

Energy 211Kcal/874kJ; Protein 8g; Carbohydrate 5.2g, of which sugars 3.4g; Fat 17.8g, of which saturates 3g; Cholesterol 95mg; Calcium 63mg; Fibre 2.8g; Sodium 51mg.

ROASTED BEETROOT WITH GARLIC SAUCE

IN GREECE, BEETROOT IS A FAVOURITE WINTER VEGETABLE, EITHER SERVED SOLO AS A SALAD OR WITH A LAYER OF THE FLAVOURFUL GARLIC SAUCE, KNOWN AS SKORDALIA, ON TOP.

SERVES FOUR

INGREDIENTS

675g/1½lb medium or small
   beetroot (beets)
75–90ml/5–6 tbsp extra virgin
   olive oil
salt

For the garlic sauce
   4 medium slices of bread, crusts
     removed, soaked in water for
     10 minutes
   2 or 3 garlic cloves, chopped
   15ml/1 tbsp white wine vinegar
   60ml/4 tbsp extra virgin
     olive oil

1 Preheat the oven to 180°C/350°F/ Gas 4. Rinse the beetroot under cold running water and rub off any grit, but be careful not to pierce the skin or the colour will run.

2 Line a roasting pan with a large sheet of foil and place the beetroot on top. Drizzle a little of the olive oil over them, sprinkle lightly with salt and fold over both edges of the foil to enclose the beetroot completely. Bake for about 1½ hours until perfectly soft.

3 Meanwhile, make the garlic sauce. Squeeze most of the water out of the soaked bread, but leave it quite moist.

4 Place the soaked bread in a blender or food processor. Add the garlic and vinegar, with salt to taste, and blend until smooth.

5 While the blender or food processor is running, drizzle in the extra virgin olive oil through the lid or feeder tube. The sauce should be runny. Spoon it into a bowl and set it aside.

6 Remove the beetroot from the foil package. When they are cool enough to handle, carefully peel them. Cut them into thin, round slices and arrange on a flat platter.

7 Drizzle with the remaining oil. Either spread a thin layer of garlic sauce on top, or hand it around separately. Serve with fresh bread, if you like.

Energy 342Kcal/1,425kJ; Protein 5g; Carbohydrate 25.2g, of which sugars 12.5g; Fat 25.4g, of which saturates 3.6g; Cholesterol 0mg; Calcium 61mg; Fibre 3.6g; Sodium 242mg.

AROMATIC BRAISED LEEKS <u>IN</u> RED WINE

CORIANDER SEEDS AND OREGANO GIVE A DELICATE FLAVOUR TO THIS DISH OF BRAISED LEEKS. SERVE IT AS PART OF A MIXED MEZE OR AS A PARTNER FOR BAKED WHITE FISH.

SERVES SIX

INGREDIENTS

12 baby leeks or 6 thick leeks
15ml/1 tbsp coriander seeds,
  lightly crushed
5cm/2in piece of cinnamon stick
120ml/4fl oz/½ cup olive oil
3 fresh bay leaves
2 strips pared orange rind
5 or 6 fresh or dried oregano sprigs
5ml/1 tsp sugar
150ml/¼ pint/⅔ cup fruity
  red wine
10ml/2 tsp balsamic or sherry vinegar
30ml/2 tbsp coarsely chopped fresh
  oregano or marjoram
salt and ground black pepper

1 If using baby leeks, simply trim the ends, but leave them whole. Cut thick leeks into 5–7.5cm/2–3in lengths.

2 Place the coriander seeds and cinnamon in a pan wide enough to take all the leeks in a single layer. Cook over a medium heat for 2–3 minutes, or until the spices give off a fragrant aroma, then stir in the olive oil, bay leaves, orange rind, fresh or dried oregano, sugar, wine and balsamic or sherry vinegar. Bring to the boil and simmer for 5 minutes.

3 Add the leeks to the pan. Bring back to the boil, reduce the heat and cover the pan. Cook the leeks gently for 5 minutes. Uncover and simmer gently for another 5–8 minutes, or until the leeks are just tender when tested with the tip of a sharp knife.

4 Use a slotted spoon to transfer the leeks to a serving dish. Boil the pan juices rapidly until reduced to about 75–90ml/5–6 tbsp. Add salt and pepper to taste and pour the liquid over the leeks. Leave to cool.

5 The leeks can be left to stand for several hours. If you chill them, bring them back to room temperature again before serving. Sprinkle the chopped herbs over the leeks just before serving.

COOK'S TIP
Balsamic vinegar is ideal for this dish. It has a high sugar content and wonderfully strong bouquet. It is a very dark brown colour and has a deep, rich flavour with hints of herbs and port. Nowadays you can find quite good balsamic vinegar in supermarkets. It is expensive, but the flavour is so rich that you only need to use a little.

Energy 151Kcal/621kJ; Protein 1.1g; Carbohydrate 1.7g, of which sugars 1.3g; Fat 13.7g, of which saturates 2g; Cholesterol 0mg; Calcium 29mg; Fibre 1.5g; Sodium 5mg.

WATERMELON AND FETA SALAD

THE COMBINATION OF SWEET WATERMELON WITH SALTY FETA CHEESE IS REFRESHING AND FLAVOURSOME. THE SALAD MAY BE SERVED PLAIN AND LIGHT, ON A LEAFY BASE. IT IS PERFECT SERVED AS AN APPETIZER OR A SIDE SALAD, OR TAKEN AS PART OF A MEZE TABLE ON A SUMMER PICNIC.

SERVES FOUR

INGREDIENTS
4 slices watermelon, chilled
130g/4½oz feta cheese, preferably
   sheep's milk feta, cut into bitesize
   pieces
handful of mixed seeds, such as
   pumpkin seeds and sunflower
   seeds, lightly toasted
10–15 black olives

COOK'S TIP
The best choice of olives for this recipe are plump black ones, such as *kalamata*, other shiny, brined varieties or dry-cured black olives.

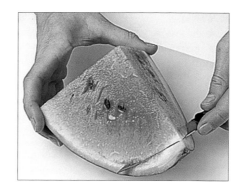

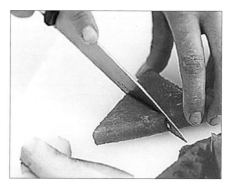

1 Cut the rind off the watermelon and remove as many seeds as possible. The sweetest and juiciest part is right in the core, and you may want to cut off any whiter flesh just under the skin.

2 Cut the flesh into triangular chunks. Mix the watermelon, feta cheese, mixed seeds and black olives. Cover and chill the salad for 30 minutes in the refrigerator before serving.

Energy 203Kcal/849kJ; Protein 7.8g; Carbohydrate 16.2g, of which sugars 14.8g; Fat 12.4g, of which saturates 5.2g; Cholesterol 23mg; Calcium 148mg; Fibre 1.1g; Sodium 754mg.

GREEK SALAD

GREEK TOMATOES ARE RIPENED IN THE SUN AND ARE ABSOLUTELY BURSTING WITH FLAVOUR. THEY MAKE THE PERFECT BASE FOR A REFRESHING SALAD WITH CUCUMBER AND THE BEST-QUALITY FETA CHEESE. USE A GOOD FRUITY EXTRA VIRGIN OLIVE OIL FOR A SUCCESSFUL SALAD.

SERVES SIX

INGREDIENTS
1 cos or romaine lettuce, sliced
450g/1lb well-flavoured tomatoes,
 cut into eighths
1 cucumber, seeded and chopped
200g/7oz feta cheese, crumbled
4 spring onions, sliced
50g/2oz/½ cup black olives, stoned
 (pitted) and halved

For the dressing
90ml/6 tbsp extra virgin olive oil
25ml/1½ tbsp lemon juice
salt and ground black pepper

1 Put the sliced lettuce, tomatoes and chopped cucumber into a large serving bowl and add the feta cheese, spring onions and black olives. Mix the ingredients together.

2 To make the dressing, mix together the extra virgin olive oil and lemon juice and season with salt and freshly ground black pepper to taste.

3 Pour the dressing over the salad. Toss the dressing into the salad well, and serve immediately with crusty bread or hot toasted pitta.

VARIATION
For a more substantial meze-style variation add red (bell) peppers, cored and chopped into bitesize pieces, and sprinkle with pine nuts if you like, and include mixed salad leaves with the lettuce.

Energy 212Kcal/879kJ; Protein 6.4g; Carbohydrate 4g, of which sugars 4g; Fat 19.1g, of which saturates 6.4g; Cholesterol 23mg; Calcium 147mg; Fibre 1.6g; Sodium 677mg.

FRIED CHEESE WITH ROCKET SALAD

AT METROPOLITAN PARTIES YOU MAY WELL BE OFFERED THIS AS FINGER FOOD, BUT THERE IS ALSO A MORE ROBUST VERSION, AS SERVED IN TAVERNAS OR PRIVATE HOMES. A SMALL, BLACKENED, CAST-IRON FRYING PAN WILL BE BROUGHT TO THE TABLE, WITH THE SLICES OF CHEESE STILL SIZZLING IN IT.

SERVES FOUR

INGREDIENTS
    30ml/2 tbsp olive oil, for frying
    8 slices Greek Kefalotiri or Greek
      Cypriot halloumi cheese, about
      1cm/½in thick
    freshly ground black pepper
    lemon wedges, to serve

For the salad
    15ml/1 tbsp red wine vinegar
    60ml/4 tbsp extra virgin olive oil
    a large handful of rocket
      (arugula) leaves

1 Start by making the salad. Whisk the vinegar and olive oil together in a bowl and dress the rocket leaves. Spread them out on a platter.

2 Heat the olive oil for frying in a large griddle pan or non-stick frying pan until hot. Lay the slices of cheese side by side on the base. Do not allow the slices to touch as they might stick together. Let them sizzle for a couple of minutes, turning each one over using tongs or a metal spatula as it starts to get crisp at the sides.

3 Sprinkle the cheese slices with pepper. As soon as the undersides turn golden, remove them from the pan and arrange them on the dressed rocket. Serve immediately, with the lemon wedges to squeeze over.

Energy 289Kcal/1,195kJ; Protein 10.7g; Carbohydrate 0.8g, of which sugars 0.8g; Fat 27g, of which saturates 9.3g; Cholesterol 29mg; Calcium 266mg; Fibre 1.1g; Sodium 268mg.

WARM HALLOUMI <u>AND</u> FENNEL SALAD

THE FIRM TEXTURE OF HALLOUMI CHEESE MAKES IT PERFECT FOR THE BARBECUE, AS IT KEEPS ITS SHAPE VERY WELL AND DOESN'T MELT IN THE SAME WAY THAT OTHER CHEESES DO. IT IS WIDELY AVAILABLE IN MOST LARGE SUPERMARKETS AND GREEK DELICATESSENS.

SERVES FOUR

INGREDIENTS
- 200g/7oz halloumi cheese, thickly sliced
- 2 fennel bulbs, trimmed and thinly sliced
- 30ml/2 tbsp roughly chopped fresh oregano
- 45ml/3 tbsp lemon-infused extra virgin olive oil
- salt and ground black pepper

COOK'S TIP

If you cannot get lemon-infused extra virgin olive oil, simply use a very fruity extra virgin olive oil and let it soak overnight with some thin slices of lemon. You can also try other flavoured oils, such as garlic or oregano, to produce a different taste.

1 Put the halloumi, fennel and oregano in a bowl and drizzle over the lemon-infused oil. Season with salt and black pepper to taste. (Halloumi is a fairly salty cheese, so be very careful when adding extra salt.)

2 Cover the bowl with clear film (plastic wrap) and chill for about 2 hours to allow the flavours to develop.

3 Remove the halloumi and fennel, reserving the marinade juices. Place on a preheated griddle pan or over the barbecue and cook for about 3 minutes on each side, until lightly charred.

4 Divide the halloumi and fennel among four serving plates and drizzle over the reserved marinade. Serve immediately with crusty bread or toasted pitta bread.

Energy 215Kcal/889kJ; Protein 10.2g; Carbohydrate 1.8g, of which sugars 1.7g; Fat 18.6g, of which saturates 8.1g; Cholesterol 29mg; Calcium 205mg; Fibre 2.4g; Sodium 209mg.

WARM BLACK-EYED BEAN SALAD <u>WITH</u> ROCKET

THIS IS A SIMPLE DISH TO MAKE, AS BLACK-EYED BEANS DO NOT NEED TO BE SOAKED OVERNIGHT. BY ADDING SPRING ONIONS AND LOADS OF AROMATIC DILL, IT IS TRANSFORMED INTO A REFRESHING AND HEALTHY SALAD. IT CAN BE SERVED HOT OR AT ROOM TEMPERATURE.

SERVES FOUR

INGREDIENTS

275g/10oz/1½ cups black-eyed
  beans (peas)
5 spring onions (scallions), sliced
  into rounds
a large handful of fresh rocket
  (arugula) leaves, chopped
  if large
45–60ml/3–4 tbsp chopped
  fresh dill
150ml/¼ pint/⅔ cup extra virgin
  olive oil
juice of 1 lemon, or to taste
10–12 black olives
salt and ground black pepper
small cos or romaine lettuce leaves,
  to serve

1 Thoroughly rinse the beans and drain them well. Tip them into a pan and pour in cold water to just about cover them. Slowly bring them to the boil over a low heat. As soon as the water is boiling, remove the pan from the heat and drain the water off immediately.

2 Put the beans back in the pan with fresh cold water to cover and add a pinch of salt – this will make their skins harder and stop them from disintegrating when they are cooked.

3 Bring the beans to the boil over a medium heat, then lower the heat and cook them until they are soft but not mushy. They will take 20–30 minutes only, so keep an eye on them.

4 Drain the beans, reserving 75–90ml/ 5–6 tbsp of the cooking liquid. Tip the beans into a large salad bowl. Immediately add the remaining ingredients, including the reserved liquid, and mix well. Serve immediately, piled on the lettuce leaves, or leave to cool slightly and serve later.

Energy 434Kcal/1,811kJ; Protein 16.6g; Carbohydrate 31.4g, of which sugars 2.7g; Fat 27.8g, of which saturates 4g; Cholesterol 0mg; Calcium 149mg; Fibre 12.5g; Sodium 334mg.

POTATO AND FETA SALAD

A POTATO SALAD MAY SOUND MUNDANE BUT THIS ONE IS NOT, AS IT IS REDOLENT WITH THE AROMAS OF THE HERBS AND HAS LAYER UPON LAYER OF FLAVOURS. IT IS AN EASY DISH TO ASSEMBLE, AND CAN ALSO MAKE FOR A PERFECT LUNCH OR A SIMPLE DINNER ON A BUSY DAY.

SERVES FOUR

INGREDIENTS

500g/1¼lb small new potatoes
5 spring onions (scallions),
  green and white parts
  finely chopped
15ml/1 tbsp rinsed bottled
  capers
8–10 black olives
115g/4oz feta cheese
45ml/3 tbsp finely chopped fresh
  flat leaf parsley
30ml/2 tbsp finely chopped
  fresh mint
salt and freshly ground
  black pepper

For the dressing
90–120ml/6–8 tbsp extra virgin
  olive oil
juice of 1 lemon, or to taste
2 salted or preserved anchovies,
  rinsed and finely chopped
45ml/3 tbsp Greek (US strained
  plain) yogurt
45ml/3 tbsp finely chopped
  fresh dill, plus a few sprigs,
  to garnish
5ml/1 tsp French mustard

1 Chop the feta cheese into small, evenly sized cubes and crumble slightly.

2 Bring a pan of lightly salted water to the boil and cook the potatoes in their skins for 25–30 minutes, or until tender. Take care not to let them become soggy and disintegrate. Drain them thoroughly and let them cool a little.

3 When the potatoes are cool enough to handle, peel them with your fingers and place them in a large bowl. If they are very small, keep them whole; otherwise cut them into large cubes. Add the chopped spring onions, capers, olives, feta cheese and fresh herbs, and toss gently to mix.

4 To make the dressing, place the extra virgin olive oil in a bowl with the lemon juice and anchovies.

5 Whisk thoroughly for a few minutes until the dressing emulsifies and thickens; you may need to add a little more olive oil if it does not thicken. Whisk in the yogurt, dill and mustard, with salt and pepper to taste.

6 Dress the salad while the potatoes are still warm, tossing lightly.

COOK'S TIP
The salad tastes better if it has had time to sit for an hour or so at room temperature and absorb all the flavours before it is served.

Energy 138Kcal/566kJ; Protein 1.3g; Carbohydrate 1.2g, of which sugars 1.1g; Fat 14.2g, of which saturates 2g; Cholesterol 0mg; Calcium 75mg; Fibre 1.4g; Sodium 40mg.

DESSERTS
AND CAKES

  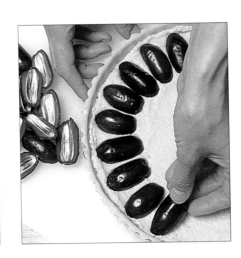

Dried and fresh fruit, nuts and, of course, the fantastically

perfumed Greek honey, combine to make the most heavenly

desserts imaginable. Cakes are traditionally eaten

throughout the day, and can also be enjoyed as

mouthwatering desserts. Delicious treats to sample include

a fruit Date and Almond Tart and a nutty Crunchy-

Topped Fresh Apricot Cake.

FRESH FIG FILO TART

FIGS COOK WONDERFULLY WELL AND TASTE SUPERB IN THIS TART — THE RIPER THE FIGS, THE BETTER. SERVE IT WITH A SPRIG OF FRESH MINT AND A FEW SPOONS OF CREAMY GREEK YOGURT.

SERVES SIX TO EIGHT

INGREDIENTS
  5 sheets filo pastry,
    35 x 25cm/14 x 10in,
    thawed if frozen
  25g/1oz/2 tbsp butter, melted, plus
    extra for greasing
  6 fresh figs, cut into wedges
  75g/3oz/⅔ cup plain
    (all-purpose) flour
  75g/3oz/6 tbsp caster
    (superfine) sugar
  4 eggs
  450ml/¾ pint/scant 2 cups
    creamy milk
  2.5ml/½ tsp almond extract
  15ml/1 tbsp icing (confectioners')
    sugar, for dusting
  whipped cream or Greek (US
    strained plain) yogurt, to serve

1 Preheat the oven to 190°C/375°F/ Gas 5. Grease a 25 x 16cm/10 x 6¼in baking tin (pan) with butter. Brush each filo sheet in turn with melted butter and use to line the prepared tin.

VARIATION
Nectarines or plums are also delicious cooked this way. Remove their stones (pits) and quarter them as for the figs.

2 Using scissors, cut off any excess pastry, leaving a little overhanging the edge. Arrange the fig wedges skin down in the filo case.

3 Sift the flour into a bowl and stir in the caster sugar. Add the eggs and a little of the milk and whisk until smooth. Gradually whisk in the remaining milk and the almond extract. Pour the mixture over the figs; bake for 1 hour, or until the batter has set and is golden.

4 Remove the tart from the oven and allow it to cool in the tin on a wire rack for 10 minutes. Dust with the icing sugar and serve with whipped cream or Greek yogurt. It will be delicious for a few days if kept refrigerated.

Energy 304Kcal/1,286kJ; Protein 9.9g; Carbohydrate 49.2g, of which sugars 30.2g; Fat 9.1g, of which saturates 4.1g; Cholesterol 140mg; Calcium 203mg; Fibre 2.3g; Sodium 118mg.

DATE AND ALMOND TART

FRESH DATES ARE POPULAR THROUGHOUT GREECE AND MAKE AN UNUSUAL BUT DELICIOUS FILLING
FOR A TART. ORANGE FLOWER WATER ADDS A DELICATE SCENT TO THE FILLING.

SERVES SIX

INGREDIENTS
175g/6oz/1½ cups plain
   (all-purpose) flour
75g/3oz/6 tbsp butter
1 egg

For the filling
90g/3½oz/7 tbsp butter
90g/3½oz/½ cup caster
   (superfine) sugar
1 egg, beaten
90g/3½oz/scant 1 cup
   ground almonds
30ml/2 tbsp plain
   (all-purpose) flour
30ml/2 tbsp orange flower water
12–13 fresh dates, halved
   and stoned (pitted)
60ml/4 tbsp apricot jam

1 Preheat the oven to 200°C/400°F/
Gas 6. Place a baking sheet in the
oven. Sift the flour into a bowl, add the
butter and work with your fingertips
until the mixture resembles fine
breadcrumbs. Add the egg and 15ml/
1 tbsp cold water, then work to a
smooth dough.

2 Roll out the pastry on a lightly floured
surface and use to line a 20cm/8in tart
pan. Prick the base with a fork, then
chill until needed.

3 To make the filling, cream the butter
and sugar until light, then beat in the
egg. Stir in the ground almonds, flour
and 15ml/1 tbsp of the orange flower
water, mixing well.

4 Spread the mixture evenly over the
base of the pastry case. Arrange the
dates, cut side down, on the almond
mixture. Bake on the hot baking sheet
for 10–15 minutes, then reduce the heat
to 180°C/350°F/Gas 4. Bake for a further
15–20 minutes until light golden and set.

5 Transfer the tart to a rack to cool.
Gently heat the apricot jam, then press
through a sieve (strainer). Add the
remaining orange flower water.

6 Brush the tart with the jam and serve
at room temperature.

Energy 478Kcal/2,003kJ; Protein 6.2g; Carbohydrate 61.1g, of which sugars 33.7g; Fat 25g, of which saturates 14.9g; Cholesterol 122mg; Calcium 82mg; Fibre 1.7g; Sodium 199mg.

NECTARINES BAKED WITH NUTS

FRESH NECTARINES STUFFED WITH A GROUND ALMOND AND CHOPPED PISTACHIO NUT FILLING ARE BAKED IN A CLAY POT UNTIL MELTINGLY TENDER, THEN SERVED WITH A PASSION FRUIT SAUCE.

SERVES FOUR

INGREDIENTS

- 50g/2oz/½ cup ground almonds
- 15ml/1 tbsp caster (superfine) sugar
- 1 egg yolk
- 50g/2oz/½ cup shelled pistachio nuts, chopped
- 4 nectarines
- 200ml/7fl oz/scant 1 cup orange juice
- 2 ripe passion fruit
- 45ml/3 tbsp Cointreau or other orange liqueur

1 Soak a small clay pot, if using, in cold water for 15 minutes. Mix the ground almonds, sugar and egg yolk to a paste, then stir in the pistachio nuts.

2 Cut the nectarines in half and carefully remove the stones (pits). Pile the ground almond and pistachio filling into the nectarine halves, packing in plenty of filling, and then place them in a single layer in the base of the clay pot or an ovenproof dish.

3 Pour the orange juice around the nectarines, then cover the pot or dish and place in an unheated oven. Set the oven to 200°C/400°F/Gas 6 and cook for 15 minutes.

4 Remove the lid from the pot or dish and bake for a further 5–10 minutes, or until the nectarines are soft. Transfer the nectarines to individual, warmed serving plates and keep warm.

5 Cut the passion fruit in half, scoop out the seeds and stir them into the cooking juices in the clay pot or dish with the liqueur. Place the nectarines on serving plates and spoon the sauce over and around them.

Energy 272Kcal/1,135kJ; Protein 7.6g; Carbohydrate 20.7g, of which sugars 20g; Fat 15.4g, of which saturates 1.9g; Cholesterol 50mg; Calcium 62mg; Fibre 3.5g; Sodium 74mg.

SEMOLINA CAKE

THIS IS A FAMILY TREAT, LOVED BY EVERYONE IN GREECE. IT IS QUICK TO MAKE AND USES INEXPENSIVE INGREDIENTS THAT MOST GREEK KITCHENS WILL HAVE IN STOCK.

SERVES SIX TO EIGHT

INGREDIENTS
500g/1¼lb/2¾ cups caster
  (superfine) sugar
1 litre/1¾ pints/4 cups cold water
1 cinnamon stick
250ml/8fl oz/1 cup olive oil
350g/12oz/2 cups coarse
  semolina
50g/2oz/½ cup blanched
  almonds
30ml/2 tbsp pine nuts
5ml/1 tsp ground cinnamon

1 Put the sugar in a heavy pan, pour in the water and add the cinnamon stick. Bring to the boil, stirring until the sugar dissolves, then boil without stirring for about 4 minutes to make a syrup.

2 Meanwhile, heat the oil in a separate, heavy pan. When it is almost smoking, add the semolina gradually and stir continuously until it turns light brown.

3 Lower the heat, add the almonds and pine nuts, and brown together for 2–3 minutes, stirring continuously. Take the semolina mixture off the heat and set aside. Remove the cinnamon stick from the hot syrup using a slotted spoon and discard it.

4 Protecting your hand with an oven glove or dish towel, carefully add the hot syrup to the semolina mixture a little at a time, stirring continuously. The mixture will probably hiss and spit at this point, so stand well away.

5 Return the pan to a gentle heat and stir until all the syrup has been absorbed and the mixture looks smooth.

6 Remove the pan from the heat, cover it with a clean dish towel and let it stand for 10 minutes so that any remaining moisture is absorbed.

7 Scrape the mixture into a 20–23cm/ 8–9in round cake tin (pan), preferably fluted, and set it aside.

8 When it is cold, unmould it on to a serving platter and dust it evenly all over with the ground cinnamon. Cut into chunky slices and serve with black coffee or tea.

COOK'S TIP
In Greece, this cake would be made with extra virgin olive oil, but you may prefer the less dominant flavour of a light olive oil.

Energy 888Kcal/3,731kJ; Protein 9.1g; Carbohydrate 133.1g, of which sugars 87.6g; Fat 39.1g, of which saturates 4.9g; Cholesterol 0mg; Calcium 75mg; Fibre 1.9g; Sodium 13mg.

LEMON AND LIME SYRUP CAKE

THIS GREEK FAVOURITE IS PERFECT FOR BUSY COOKS AS IT CAN BE MIXED IN MOMENTS AND NEEDS NO ICING. THE SIMPLE TANGY LIME TOPPING TRANSFORMS IT INTO A FABULOUSLY MOIST CAKE.

SERVES EIGHT

INGREDIENTS
225g/8oz/2 cups self-raising
(self-rising) flour
5ml/1 tsp baking powder
225g/8oz/generous 1 cup caster
(superfine) sugar
225g/8oz/1 cup butter, softened
4 eggs, beaten
grated rind of 2 lemons
30ml/2 tbsp lemon juice

For the topping
finely pared rind of 1 lime
juice of 2 limes
150g/5oz/⅔ cup caster sugar

1 Preheat the oven to 160°C/325°F/ Gas 3. Grease and line a 20cm/8in round cake tin (pan). Sift the flour and baking powder into a bowl.

2 Add the caster sugar, butter and eggs, and beat thoroughly. Then gradually add and beat in the lemon rind and juice. Spoon the mixture into the prepared tin, then smooth the surface and make a shallow indentation in the top with the back of a spoon.

3 Bake for 1¼–1½ hours, or until the cake is golden and a skewer inserted in the centre comes out clean.

4 Meanwhile, mix the topping ingredients together in a small bowl. As soon as the cake is cooked, remove it from the oven and pour the topping evenly over the surface. Allow the cake to cool in the tin.

VARIATION
Use lemon rind and juice instead of lime for the topping if you prefer. You will need only one large lemon.

Energy 524Kcal/2,197kJ; Protein 6g; Carbohydrate 70.4g, of which sugars 49.5g; Fat 26.2g, of which saturates 15.5g; Cholesterol 155mg; Calcium 143mg; Fibre 0.9g; Sodium 310mg.

CRUNCHY-TOPPED FRESH APRICOT CAKE

ALMONDS ARE PERFECT PARTNERS FOR FRESH APRICOTS, AND THIS IS A GREAT WAY TO USE UP FIRM FRUITS. IN GREECE THIS IS SERVED AS A CAKE OR SNACK TO BE EATEN THROUGHOUT THE DAY.

SERVES EIGHT

INGREDIENTS
175g/6oz/1½ cups self-raising (self-rising) flour
175g/6oz/¾ cup butter, softened
175g/6oz/scant 1 cup caster (superfine) sugar
115g/4oz/1 cup ground almonds
3 eggs
5ml/1 tsp almond extract
2.5ml/½ tsp baking powder
8 firm apricots, stoned (pitted) and chopped

For the topping
30ml/2 tbsp demerara (raw) sugar
50g/2oz/½ cup flaked (sliced) almonds

1 Preheat the oven to 160°C/325°F/ Gas 3. Grease an 18cm/7in round cake tin (pan). Cut out a round of baking parchment to fit the cake tin and line it carefully into the corners.

2 Put all the cake ingredients, except the apricots, in a large mixing bowl and whisk until creamy. Fold the apricots into the cake mixture.

3 Spoon into the tin. Make a hollow in the centre with the back of a spoon. Sprinkle 15ml/1 tbsp of the demerara sugar over with the flaked almonds.

4 Bake for 1½ hours or until an inserted skewer comes out clean. Sprinkle the remaining sugar over and cool for 10 minutes in the tin. Remove from the tin and cool on a wire rack.

Energy 414Kcal/1,734kJ; Protein 6.2g; Carbohydrate 46.8g, of which sugars 30.3g; Fat 23.9g, of which saturates 12.3g; Cholesterol 118mg; Calcium 126mg; Fibre 1.8g; Sodium 241mg.

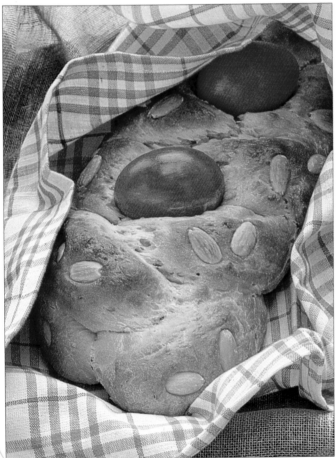

SWEETS, COOKIES AND BREADS

The Greeks love to celebrate special occasions with all kinds of special sweets, cookies and breads, and these often vary from region to region. Here, you will find a selection of festive treats to try, such as Christmas Honey Cookies and Greek Easter Bread. Teatime delights include Fruit and Nut Pastries, and Loukoumia, and there are savoury options too, such as Pitta and Spring Onion Flatbreads.

LOUKOUMIA

THIS IS THE GREEK VERSION OF TURKISH DELIGHT AND THIS VERSATILE RECIPE IS MADE ALL OVER THE COUNRTY. SERVE A FEW CUBES WITH COFFEE AFTER A HEAVY MEAL, FOR A PICK-ME-UP. YOU CAN PUT COCKTAIL STICKS IN EACH PIECE AND DECORATE WITH A SPRINKLING OF ICING SUGAR.

MAKES 450G/1LB

INGREDIENTS
   400g/14oz/2 cups sugar
   300ml/½ pint/1¼ cups water
   25g/1oz powdered gelatine
   2.5ml/½ tsp cream of tartar
   30ml/2 tbsp rose water
   pink food colouring
   45ml/3 tbsp icing (confectioners')
     sugar, sifted
   15ml/1 tbsp cornflour (cornstarch)

VARIATION
Try different flavours in this recipe, such as lemon, crème de menthe and orange and then vary the food colouring accordingly. For a truly authentic touch, add some chopped pistachio nuts to the mixture before pouring it into the tins.

1 Slightly dampen the insides of two 18cm/7in shallow square tins (pans) with lukewarm water – be sure not to wet them too much. Place the sugar and all but 60ml/4 tbsp of the water in a heavy pan. Heat gently over a low heat, stirring occasionally, until the sugar has completely dissolved.

2 Blend the gelatine and remaining water in a small bowl and place the mixture in a small pan. Heat gently over a low heat, stirring frequently, to dissolve the gelatine completely.

3 Bring the sugar syrup to the boil and boil steadily for about 8 minutes until the syrup registers 130°C/260°F on a sugar thermometer.

4 Stir the cream of tartar into the gelatine, then pour into the boiling syrup and stir until well blended. Remove from the heat.

5 Add the rose water and a few drops of pink food colouring to tint the mixture pale pink. Pour the mixture into the tins and allow to set for several hours or overnight, if possible.

6 Dust a sheet of waxed paper or baking parchment with some of the icing sugar and cornflour. Dip the base of the tin in hot water. Invert on to the paper. Cut into 2.5cm/1in squares using an oiled knife.

Energy 1,806Kcal/7,707kJ; Protein 2.3g; Carbohydrate 478.8g, of which sugars 465g; Fat 0.1g, of which saturates 0g; Cholesterol 0mg; Calcium 238mg; Fibre 0g; Sodium 35mg.

ORANGE SPOON PRESERVE

SPOON PRESERVES ARE MADE WITH VARIOUS TYPES OF FRUIT IN A LUSCIOUS SYRUP. FIGS, CHERRIES, GRAPES AND APRICOTS ARE ALL SUITABLE, AS ARE SMALL BITTER ORANGES, WHICH ARE LEFT WHOLE. THERE IS ALSO A BEAUTIFUL PRESERVE WHICH IS MADE FROM ROSE PETALS.

MAKES ABOUT THIRTY PIECES

INGREDIENTS
   8 or 9 thick-skinned oranges, total
     weight about 1kg/2¼lb, rinsed
     and dried
   1kg/2¼lb/5¼ cups caster
     (superfine) sugar
   juice of 1 lemon

1 Grate the oranges lightly and discard the zest. Slice each one vertically into 4–6 pieces (depending on the size of the oranges), remove the peel from each segment, keeping it in one piece, and drop it into a bowl of cold water. Use the flesh in another recipe.

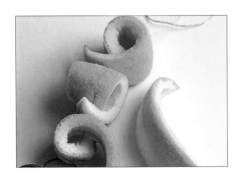

2 Have ready a tapestry needle threaded with strong cotton string. Roll up a piece of peel and push the needle through it so that it is threaded on the string. Continue this process until there are 10–12 pieces on the string, then tie the two ends together.

3 Put the strings in a bowl of fresh cold water and leave for 24 hours, changing the water 3–4 times.

4 Next day, drain the strings of peel and put them in a large pan. Pour in about 2.8 litres/5 pints/12½ cups water. Bring to the boil, partially cover the pan and continue to boil for 15 minutes. Drain well. Return the strings of peel to the pan, cover with the same amount of water and boil for a further 10 minutes, or until the peel feels soft but is not overcooked or disintegrating. Tip them into a colander and leave to drain for at least 1 hour.

5 Put the sugar in a large, heavy pan and add 150ml/¼ pint/⅔ cup water. Stir over a gentle heat until the sugar dissolves, then boil gently without stirring for about 4 minutes until it forms a thick syrup.

6 Release the fruit into the syrup by cutting the threads. Simmer for 5 minutes, then remove the pan from the heat and leave the cooked peel to stand in the syrup overnight.

7 Next day, boil the syrup very gently for 4–5 minutes, until it starts to set. Stir in the lemon juice, take the pan off the heat and let the preserve cool. Pack the curled peel and syrup into sterilized jars. Seal and label, then store in a cool, dry place.

HOW TO SERVE
This type of spoon preserve – glyko tou *koutaliou* – is often served to visitors. Offer one piece on a spoon, resting in a saucer, along with a glass of cold water.

Energy 131Kcal/560kJ; Protein 0.3g; Carbohydrate 34.8g, of which sugars 34.8g; Fat 0g, of which saturates 0g; Cholesterol 0mg; Calcium 31mg; Fibre 0g; Sodium 3mg.

CHRISTMAS HONEY COOKIES

DELICIOUS, HONEY-COATED MELOMAKARONA *ARE A TREAT SPECIALLY MADE DURING THE*
CHRISTMAS PERIOD. THEY ARE EASY TO MAKE AND TASTE SIMPLY MARVELLOUS.

MAKES TWENTY

INGREDIENTS
   2.5ml/½ tsp bicarbonate of soda
   (baking soda)
   grated rind and juice of 1 large orange
   150ml/¼ pint/⅔ cup extra virgin
   olive oil
   75g/3oz/6 tbsp caster (superfine) sugar
   60ml/4 tbsp brandy
   7.5ml/1½ tsp ground cinnamon
   400g/14oz/3½ cups self-raising
   (self-rising) flour sifted with a
   pinch of salt
   115g/4oz/1 cup shelled
   walnuts, chopped

For the syrup
   225g/8oz/1 cup clear honey
   115g/4oz/½ cup caster
   (superfine) sugar

1 Mix together the baking soda and orange juice. Beat the oil and sugar with an electric mixer until blended. Beat in the brandy and 2.5ml/½ tsp of the cinnamon, then add and beat in the orange juice and soda.

2 Using your hand, gradually work the flour and salt into the mixture. As soon as it becomes possible to do so, knead it. Add the orange rind and knead for 10 minutes or until the dough is pliable.

3 Preheat the oven to 180°C/350°F/ Gas 4. Flour your hands and pinch off small pieces of the dough. Shape them into 6cm/2½in long ovals and place on ungreased baking sheets.

4 Using a fork dipped in water, flatten each oval of dough a little. Bake for 25 minutes, or until golden. Cool slightly, then transfer to a wire rack to harden.

5 Meanwhile, make the syrup. Place the honey, sugar and 150ml/¼ pint/⅔ cup water in a small pan. Bring gently to the boil, stirring continuously. Then skim any surface foam, lower the heat and simmer for 5 minutes.

6 Immerse the cold *melomakarona* about six at a time into the hot syrup and leave them cooking for about 1–2 minutes.

7 Lift them out with a slotted spoon and place on a platter in a single layer. Sprinkle with the chopped walnuts and remaining cinnamon.

Energy 173Kcal/724kJ; Protein 2.7g; Carbohydrate 19.5g, of which sugars 4.6g; Fat 9.2g, of which saturates 1.1g; Cholesterol 0mg; Calcium 78mg; Fibre 0.8g; Sodium 73mg.

BUTTER <u>AND</u> ALMOND SHORTBREADS

DAZZLING WHITE KOURABIEDES ARE TRADITIONALLY MADE AT CHRISTMAS AND EASTER, BUT ARE ALSO AN IMPORTANT FEATURE OF MANY OTHER GREEK CELEBRATIONS.

MAKES TWENTY TO TWENTY-TWO

INGREDIENTS
225g/8oz/1 cup unsalted butter
150g/5oz/²⁄₃ cup caster
(superfine) sugar
2 egg yolks
5ml/1 tsp vanilla extract
2.5ml/½ tsp bicarbonate of soda
(baking soda)
45ml/3 tbsp brandy
500g/1¼lb/5 cups plain (all-purpose)
flour sifted with a pinch of salt
150g/5oz/1¼ cups blanched
almonds, toasted and
coarsely chopped
350g/12oz/3 cups icing
(confectioners') sugar

1 Cream the butter and beat in the caster sugar gradually, until light and fluffy. Beat in the egg yolks one at a time, then the vanilla.

2 Mix the soda with the brandy and stir into the mixture. Add the flour and salt and mix to a firm dough. Knead lightly, add the almonds and knead again.

3 Preheat the oven to 180°C/350°F/ Gas 4. Cover half the dough with clear film (plastic wrap) and set aside. Roll out the remaining dough until about 2.5cm/1in thick. Press out star or half-moon shapes, using pastry cutters. Repeat with the remaining dough.

4 Place the shapes on the baking sheets and bake for 20–25 minutes, or until pale golden. Do not let them brown.

5 Meanwhile, sift a quarter of the icing sugar on to a platter. As soon as the *kourabiethes* come out of the oven, dust them generously with icing sugar. Let them cool for a few minutes, then place them on the sugar-coated platter. Sift the remaining icing sugar over them, making them pure white.

Energy 324Kcal/1,363kJ; Protein 4.4g; Carbohydrate 46.1g, of which sugars 26.9g; Fat 14.3g, of which saturates 6.4g; Cholesterol 44mg; Calcium 71mg; Fibre 1.3g; Sodium 72mg.

FRUIT AND NUT PASTRIES

AROMATIC SWEET PASTRY CRESCENTS, KNOWN AS MOSHOPOUNGIA IN GREECE, ARE PACKED WITH CANDIED CITRUS PEEL AND WALNUTS, WHICH HAVE BEEN SOAKED IN A COFFEE SYRUP.

MAKES SIXTEEN

INGREDIENTS
    60ml/4 tbsp clear honey
    60ml/4 tbsp strong brewed coffee
    75g/3oz/½ cup mixed candied citrus
      peel, finely chopped
    175g/6oz/1½ cups walnuts, chopped
    1.5ml/¼ tsp freshly grated nutmeg
    milk, to glaze
    caster (superfine) sugar, for sprinkling

For the pastry
    450g/1lb/4 cups plain (all purpose)
      flour
    2.5ml/½ tsp ground cinnamon
    2.5ml/½ tsp baking powder
    pinch of salt
    150g/5oz/10 tbsp butter
    30ml/2 tbsp caster
      (superfine) sugar
    1 egg
    120ml/4fl oz/½ cup chilled milk

1 Preheat the oven to 180°C/350°F/ Gas 4. To make the pastry, sift the flour, cinnamon, baking powder and salt into a bowl. Rub or cut in the butter until the mixture resembles breadcrumbs. Stir in the sugar. Make a well.

2 Beat the egg and milk together and pour into the well in the dry ingredients. Mix to a soft dough. Divide the dough into two and wrap each piece in clear film (plastic wrap). Chill for 30 minutes.

3 Meanwhile, mix the honey and coffee in a mixing bowl. Add the candied peel, walnuts and nutmeg. Stir well, cover and leave for 20 minutes.

4 Roll out one portion of the dough on a lightly floured surface to a thickness of 3mm/⅛in. Stamp out rounds, using a 10cm/4in plain pastry cutter.

5 Place a heaped teaspoonful of filling on one side of each round. Brush the edges with a little milk, then fold over and press together to seal. Repeat with the second piece of pastry until all the filling has been used.

6 Place the pastries on lightly greased baking sheets, brush lightly over the whole top surface of each pastry with a little milk, and then sprinkle with a little caster sugar. Make a steam hole in the centre of each pastry with a skewer. Bake for 35 minutes, or until slightly puffy and lightly browned. Cool on a wire rack, and serve with coffee or tea.

VARIATION
Instead of the walnuts, use pecan nuts or almonds, if you prefer.

Energy 278Kcal/1,162kJ; Protein 5g; Carbohydrate 30.2g, of which sugars 8.7g; Fat 16.1g, of which saturates 5.7g; Cholesterol 32mg; Calcium 69mg; Fibre 1.5g; Sodium 80mg.

OLIVE BREAD

RICH OLIVE BREADS ARE POPULAR ALL OVER THE MEDITERRANEAN. FOR THIS GREEK RECIPE USE RICH OILY OLIVES OR THOSE MARINATED IN HERBS, RATHER THAN CANNED ONES.

MAKES TWO 675G/1½LB LOAVES

INGREDIENTS

    2 red onions, thinly sliced
    30ml/2 tbsp extra virgin olive oil
    225g/8oz/2 cups pitted black or
      green olives
    800g/1¾lb/7 cups strong white
      bread flour
    7.5ml/1½ tsp salt
    20ml/4 tsp easy-blend (rapid-rise)
      dried yeast
    45ml/3 tbsp each roughly chopped
      fresh flat leaf parsley, coriander
      (cilantro) or mint

1 Fry the onions in the oil until soft. Roughly chop the olives.

2 Put the flour, salt, yeast and parsley, coriander or mint in a large bowl with the olives and fried onions and pour in 475ml/16fl oz/2 cups hand-hot water.

3 Mix to a dough using a round-bladed knife, adding a little more water if the mixture feels dry. Turn out on to a lightly floured surface and knead for about 10 minutes.

4 Put in a clean bowl, cover with clear film (plastic wrap) and leave in a warm place until doubled in bulk.

5 Preheat the oven to 220°C/425°F/ Gas 7. Lightly grease two baking sheets. Turn the dough on to a floured surface and cut in half. Shape each half into a round and place both on the baking sheets. Cover loosely with lightly oiled clear film and leave in a warm place until doubled in size.

VARIATION
You can make individual rolls. Shape the dough into 16 small rolls. Slash the tops as above and reduce the cooking time to 25 minutes.

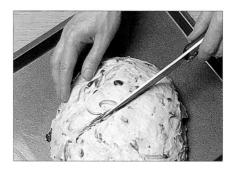

6 Slash the tops of the loaves with a knife and then bake in the oven for about 40 minutes, or until the loaves are golden brown and sound hollow when tapped on the bottom. Transfer to a wire rack to cool. Serve with fresh unsalted Greek butter or as part of a meze table with a Greek salad.

Energy 1,546Kcal/6,538kJ; Protein 38.5g; Carbohydrate 301.9g, of which sugars 13.2g; Fat 28.8g, of which saturates 4.3g; Cholesterol 0mg; Calcium 671mg; Fibre 17.8g; Sodium 4,028mg.

CHRISTOPSOMO

*A BYZANTINE CROSS FLAVOURED WITH ANISEED TOPS THIS GREEK CHRISTMAS BREAD, WHICH IS ALSO
DECORATED WITH WALNUTS FOR GOOD FORTUNE. THE FLUFFY, LIGHT, BUTTER-ENRICHED BREAD CONTAINS
ORANGE RIND, CINNAMON AND CLOVES — ALL THE LOVELY WARM TASTES ASSOCIATED WITH CHRISTMAS.*

2 Beat the eggs and sugar until light
and fluffy. Beat into the yeast mixture.
Gradually mix in the remaining flour and
salt. Beat in the softened butter and
knead to a soft but not sticky dough.
Knead on a lightly floured surface for
8–10 minutes until smooth and elastic.
Place in a lightly oiled bowl, cover with
lightly oiled clear film and leave to rise
in a warm place for 1½ hours, or until
doubled in bulk.

3 Turn out on to a lightly floured surface
and gently knock back (punch down).
Cut off about 50g/2oz of dough; cover
and set aside. Gently knead the orange
rind, cinnamon and cloves into the large
piece of dough and shape into a round
loaf. Place on the baking sheet.

4 Knead the aniseed into the remaining
dough. Cut the dough in half and shape
each piece into a 30cm/12in-long rope.
Cut through each rope at either end by
one-third of its length. Place the two
ropes in a cross on top of the loaf, then
curl each cut end into a circle, in
opposite directions.

5 Place a walnut half inside each circle.
Cover the loaf with lightly oiled clear
film and leave to rise for 45 minutes, or
until doubled in size.

MAKES ONE LOAF

INGREDIENTS
   15g/½oz fresh yeast
   140ml/scant ¼ pint/scant ⅔ cup
     lukewarm milk
   450g/1lb/4 cups unbleached strong
     white bread flour
   2 eggs
   75g/3oz/6 tbsp caster (superfine) sugar
   2.5ml/½ tsp salt
   75g/3oz/6 tbsp butter, softened
   grated rind of ½ orange
   5ml/1 tsp ground cinnamon
   1.5ml/¼ tsp ground cloves
   pinch of crushed aniseed
   8 walnut halves
   beaten egg white, for glazing

1 Lightly grease a large baking sheet. In
a large bowl, mix the yeast with the milk
until the yeast is dissolved, then stir in
115g/4oz/1 cup of the flour to make a
thin batter. Cover with lightly oiled clear
film (plastic wrap) and leave to "sponge"
in a warm place for 30 minutes.

6 Preheat the oven to 190°C/375°F/Gas
5. Brush the bread with the egg white
and bake for 40–45 minutes, or until
golden. Cool on a wire rack and then
refrigerate. You can keep it refrigerated
for up to a week.

Energy 2,840Kcal/11,958kJ; Protein 65.5g; Carbohydrate 436.2g, of which sugars 93.1g; Fat 105g, of which saturates 46.5g; Cholesterol 549mg; Calcium 941mg; Fibre 15.2g; Sodium 1,658mg.

GREEK EASTER BREAD

IN GREECE, EASTER CELEBRATIONS ARE VERY IMPORTANT, AND INVOLVE MUCH PREPARATION IN THE KITCHEN. THIS BREAD IS SOLD IN ALL THE BAKERS' SHOPS, AND ALSO MADE AT HOME. IT IS TRADITIONALLY DECORATED WITH RED-DYED EGGS.

MAKES ONE LOAF

INGREDIENTS
    25g/1oz fresh yeast
    120ml/4fl oz/½ cup warm milk
    675g/1½lb/6 cups strong white
        bread flour
    2 eggs, beaten
    2.5ml/½ tsp caraway seeds
    15ml/1 tbsp caster
        (superfine) sugar
    15ml/1 tbsp brandy
    50g/2oz/¼ cup butter, melted
    1 egg white, beaten
    2 or 3 hard-boiled eggs, dyed red
    50g/2oz/½ cup split almonds

4 Preheat the oven to 180°C/350°F/ Gas 4. Knock back (punch down) the dough and knead on a floured surface for a minute or two. Divide it into three, and roll each piece into a long sausage. Make a braid as shown above.

5 Place the loaf on a greased baking sheet. Tuck the ends under, brush with the egg white and decorate with the dyed eggs and split almonds.

6 Bake for about 1 hour, until the loaf sounds hollow when tapped on the bottom. Serve while it is still hot, or cool on a wire rack and serve cold with butter, Greek (US strained plain) yoghurt, assorted nuts and fresh and dried fruits.

COOK'S TIP
You can often buy fresh yeast from bakers' shops. It should be pale cream in colour with a firm but crumbly texture.

1 Crumble the yeast into a bowl. Mix with 15–30ml/1–2 tbsp warm water, until softened. Add the milk and 115g/4oz/ 1 cup of the flour and mix to a creamy consistency. Cover with a cloth, and leave in a warm place to rise for 1 hour.

2 Sift the remaining flour into a large bowl and make a well in the centre. Pour the risen yeast into the well, and draw in a little of the flour from the sides. Add the eggs, caraway seeds, sugar and brandy. Incorporate the remaining flour, until the mixture begins to form a dough.

3 Mix in the melted butter. Turn on to a floured surface, and knead for about 10 minutes, or until the dough becomes smooth. Return to the bowl, and cover with a cloth. Leave in a warm place to rise for 3 hours.

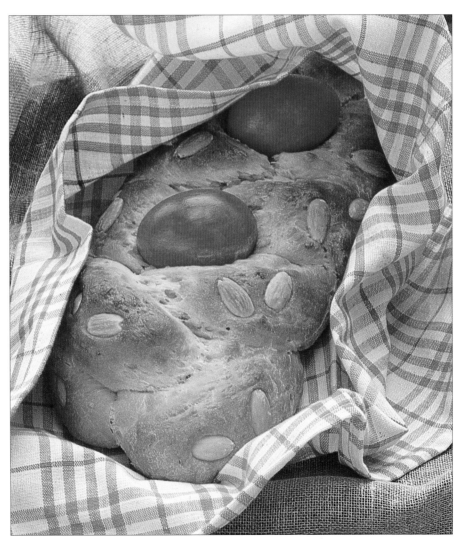

Energy 3,286Kcal/13,869kJ; Protein 93.8g; Carbohydrate 549.5g, of which sugars 33.8g; Fat 90.9g, of which saturates 34g; Cholesterol 494mg; Calcium 1,285mg; Fibre 24.6g; Sodium 584mg.

PITTA BREAD

SOFT, SLIGHTLY BUBBLY PITTA BREAD IS A PLEASURE TO MAKE. IT CAN BE EATEN IN A VARIETY OF WAYS, SUCH AS FILLED WITH SALAD OR LITTLE CHUNKS OF BARBECUED MEAT.

MAKES TWELVE

INGREDIENTS
   500g/1¼lb/5 cups strong
     white bread flour, or half
     white and half wholemeal
     (whole-wheat)
   12.5ml/2½ tsp easy-blend
     (rapid-rise) dried yeast
   15ml/1 tbsp salt
   15ml/1 tbsp olive oil

1 Combine the flour, yeast and salt. Combine the olive oil and 250ml/8fl oz/1 cup water, then add the flour mixture, stirring in the same direction, and then working with your hands until the dough is stiff. Place the dough in a clean bowl, cover with a clean dish towel and leave in a warm place for at least 30 minutes and up to 2 hours.

2 Knead the dough for 10 minutes, or until smooth. Lightly oil the bowl, place the dough in it, cover again and leave to rise in a warm place for about 1 hour, or until doubled in size.

3 Divide the dough into 12 equal pieces. With lightly floured hands, flatten each piece, then roll out into a round measuring about 20cm/8in and about ½–1cm/¼–½in thick.

4 Heat a heavy frying pan over a medium-high heat. When hot, lay one piece of flattened dough in the pan and cook for 15–20 seconds. Turn it over and cook the second side for about 1 minute.

5 When large bubbles start to form on the bread, which should be after about 1–2 minutes or so, turn it over again. It should puff up. Using a clean dish towel, gently press on the bread where the bubbles have formed. Cook the bread for a total of 3 minutes, then remove the pitta from the pan. Repeat with the remaining dough.

6 Wrap the pitta breads in a clean dish towel, stacking them as each one is cooked. Serve the pittas hot while they are soft and moist, with a main meal, such as lamb kebabs, or as part of a meze table.

VARIATION
To bake the breads, preheat the oven to 220°C/425°F/Gas 7. Fill an unglazed or partially glazed dish with hot water and place in the bottom of the hot oven. Alternatively, arrange a handful of unglazed tiles in the base of the oven. Use either a non-stick baking sheet or a lightly oiled baking sheet and heat in the oven for a few minutes. Place two or three pieces of flattened dough on to the hot baking sheet and place in the hottest part of the oven. Bake for 2–3 minutes, or until puffed up. Repeat with the remaining dough.

Energy 150Kcal/638kJ; Protein 3.9g; Carbohydrate 32.4g, of which sugars 0.6g; Fat 1.5g, of which saturates 0.2g; Cholesterol 0mg; Calcium 58mg; Fibre 1.3g; Sodium 165mg.

SPRING ONION FLATBREADS

USE THESE FLATBREADS TO WRAP AROUND BARBECUE-COOKED MEAT AND CHUNKY VEGETABLE SALADS, OR SERVE WITH TASTY DIPS SUCH AS HUMMUS. THEY'RE AT THEIR BEST AS SOON AS THEY'RE COOKED.

MAKES SIXTEEN

INGREDIENTS
    450g/1lb/4 cups strong white bread
      flour, plus extra for dusting
    5ml/1 tsp salt
    7g/¼oz packet easy-blend (rapid-rise)
      dried yeast
    4 spring onions (scallions),
      finely chopped

1 Place the flour in a large mixing bowl and stir in the salt, yeast and spring onions. Make a well in the centre and pour in 300ml/½ pint/1¼ cups hand-hot water. Mix to form a soft, but not sticky, dough.

2 Turn out the dough on to a floured work surface and knead for about 5 minutes, until smooth.

3 Put the dough back in the bowl, cover with a damp dish towel and leave in a warm place until doubled in size.

4 Knock back (punch down) the dough to get rid of any excess air, and turn it out on to a floured work surface or board. Divide the dough into 16 pieces and roll each piece into a smooth ball. Roll out each ball to flatten it to a 13cm/5in round.

5 Heat a large frying pan until hot. Dust off any excess flour from one dough round and cook for 1 minute, until slightly browned in parts, then flip over and cook for 30 seconds. Repeat with the remaining dough rounds.

VARIATION
To make garlic flatbreads, use 2 finely chopped garlic cloves in place of the spring onions (scallions).

Energy 97Kcal/410kJ; Protein 2.7g; Carbohydrate 21.9g, of which sugars 0.5g; Fat 0.4g, of which saturates 0.1g; Cholesterol 0mg; Calcium 40mg; Fibre 0.9g; Sodium 124mg.

INDEX